RE
LE

Strategies for Lean
Management Success

Bob Emiliani

Volume Five

The Center for Lean Business Management, LLC
Wethersfield, Connecticut

The CLBM, LLC
Wethersfield, CT
Tel: 860.558.7367   www.bobemiliani.com

Cover design and page layout by Tom Bittel, bittelworks@sbcglobal.net
www.dadsnoisybasement.com

Library of Congress Control Number: 2009907257
Emiliani, M.L., 1958-
    REAL LEAN: Strategies for Lean Management Success
    (Volume Five) / M.L. Emiliani

Includes bibliographical references and index
1. Business 2. Lean management 3. Leadership

I. Title
ISBN-13: 978-0-9722591-9-4

First Edition   January 2010

Ordering information
www.bobemiliani.com

Made in the U.S.A. using print-on-demand technology.

Books by M.L. "Bob" Emiliani

Better Thinking, Better Results: Case Study and Analysis of an Enterprise-Wide Lean Transformation

Practical Lean Leadership: A Strategic Leadership Guide for Executives

REAL LEAN: Understanding the Lean Management System (Volume One)

REAL LEAN: Critical Issues and Opportunities in Lean Management (Volume Two)

REAL LEAN: The Keys to Sustaining Lean Management (Volume Three)

REAL LEAN: Learning the Craft of Lean Management (Volume Four)

Principles of Mass and Flow Production
by F. G. Woollard, 55th Anniversary Special Reprint Edition

Journal Papers by M.L. "Bob" Emiliani

"Standardized Work for Executive Leadership"

"Origins of Lean Management in America:
The Role of Connecticut Businesses"

"Leaders Lost in Transformation"

"Using Value Stream Maps to Improve Leadership"

"Linking Leaders' Beliefs to Their
Behaviors and Competencies"

"Cracking the Code of Business"

"Lean Behaviors"

"Continuous Personal Improvement"

"Using Kaizen to Improve Graduate
Business School Degree Programs"

"Improving Business School Courses by
Applying Lean Principles and Practices"

"Improving Management Education"

To the value-adders, who deserve greater
respect from management and society.

Preface

I thought that I had completed the *REAL LEAN* series of books when I finished writing the fourth volume. I realized soon thereafter that the series was not yet complete and that there were more questions that needed to be answered. In addition, I was encouraged by readers to continue writing.

The feedback I receive from readers often centers upon how the *REAL LEAN* series of books explains Lean management in ways that no other books do. Readers recognize the *REAL LEAN* books as highly original and creative works that are useful for hands-on Lean practitioners. I hope I have succeeded in doing this once again as I present to you the fifth volume, *REAL LEAN: Strategies for Lean Management Success.*

Upon reflection over my many years of Lean practice, teaching Lean management, studying the history of Lean management, and educating executives to become Lean leaders, I have learned that the vast majority of executives have little interest in management history; they do not analyze the failures of other companies; they are detached and have difficulty seeing reality at the ground-level; they do not utilize internal and external human resources well; and they have very little confidence in their ability to become self-reliant in their Lean journey.

These five problems contribute greatly to the many difficulties that most companies have in their Lean transformation. They also constitute a set of strategies that can help executives become more successful Lean leaders:

- Pay Attention to History
- Learn From Others
- See Reality
- Work Together
- Change Your World

This book contains essays that relate to each of the five strategies. The essays are not meant to be a comprehensive discussion of each strategy. Rather, the essays are meant to illustrate the importance of each of the five strategies and provide specific, practical, and actionable information. They are also meant to stimulate readers to do additional self-study pertaining to each of the five strategies.

In addition, I hope that you will consider re-reading the prior four volumes of *REAL LEAN* in the context of this set of strategies. I think you will find it worthwhile to do so.

I hope I have been successful at answering new questions, and also inspiring readers to continue to educate themselves about Lean management through books and daily application of Lean principles and practices.

Will there be a sixth volume of *REAL LEAN*? Who knows; that depends on if there are new substantive questions that need to be answered. You can participate in this process by sending me an e-mail with the problems that you see related to Lean leadership, Lean transformation, or the Lean management system.

Finally, my tone in this volume, as in all the others, is very direct. Please do not be offended by my sharp comments. My intent is simply to lay facts bare and to help Lean management practitioners succeed.

Bob Emiliani
December 2009
Wethersfield, Conn.

Contents

1 Pay Attention to History

Lean management as we know it today was created through an evolutionary process beginning in the late 1880s. The early pioneers of progressive management were Frederick Taylor, Frank Gilbreth, Henry Ford, and Frank Woollard. Executives who are serious about Lean management should read the books and papers written by these practical businessmen. Studying their work will make it clear that the problems managers face today are almost exactly the same as the problems faced by earlier generations of managers.

It will also help managers avoid making two critical, erroneous assumptions. The first is:

- Thinking that your experience is unique.

While on some level our experiences are unique, such as today's computerized information systems versus yesterday's triplicate forms and manual filing systems. On other, more basic levels, the challenges of strategic management and day-to-day execution remain largely unchanged, and therefore the experiences of today's managers are far from unique. There is much to learn from those who have previously traveled the road you are now on.

The second erroneous assumption is:

- People before us figured things out.

We assume that the business processes, policies, and metrics that are in use today were carefully scrutinized by smart people long ago to ensure they are appropriate and helpful for conducting business and achieving important goals. Instead, we should assume that business processes, policies, and metrics were poorly scrutinized and simply carried over from one generation of managers to the next because that is easier to do. Executives, working on and with kaizen teams, have to examine each business process, policy, and metric, one-by-one, to determine if they support or contradict Lean principles and practices.

Ignoring the history of progressive management means executives will repeat mistakes. This is costly, time-consuming, and unnecessary, and is also inconsistent with both the "Continuous Improvement" and "Respect for People" principles in Lean management. Do not ignore history.

Eighteen Principles of Flow Production

Frank G. Woollard, the long-forgotten 1920s British pioneer of flow production, made many unique contributions including the establishment of 18 principles of flow production. Woollard recognized that flow necessarily drives everyone to the same principles and eventually to the same practices as well. Knowing this can help us avoid the perennial problem in Lean management of periodically re-discovering that which was previously done so well but has been forgotten.

In his book *Principles of Mass and Flow Production* [1], published in 1954, Frank G. Woollard said: "When setting up a flow production plant there are certain basic principles that must be obeyed. They are all simple and virtually axiomatic..." Mr. Woollard identified 18 principles, listed below, all of which relate directly to our current day understanding of Lean production.

His book, republished in January 2009 as a 55th Anniversary Special Reprint Edition [2], explains each one of the 18 principles in detail. It is well worth reading to understand the 18 principles and also to recognize Woollard's many important contributions to flow production, industrial management, and automation, between the time of Henry Ford in the United States and Kiichiro Toyoda in Japan.

Later in 1954, Woollard wrote a 22-page booklet titled: *Flow Production and Automation: Eighteen Axioms* [3]. In that booklet he said: "There are certain conditions which are necessary to the introduction of the flow-line system of production. These are axiomatic and it is essential that they be

Woollard's Principles of Flow Production

#	Principle	#	Principle
1.	a) Mass production demands mass consumption. b) Flow production requires continuity of demand.	10.	Operations must be based on motion study and time study.
2.	The products of the system must be specialized.	11.	Accuracy of work must be strictly maintained.
3.	The products of the system must be standardized.	12.	Long-term planning, based on precise knowledge, is essential.
4.	The products of the system must be simplified in general and in detail.	13.	Maintenance must be by anticipation – never by default.
5.	All material supplies must conform to specification.	14.	Every mechanical aid must be adopted for man and machine.
6.	All supplies must be delivered to strict timetable.	15.	Every activity must be studied for the economic application of power.
7.	The machines must be continually fed with sound material.	16.	Information on costs must be promptly available.
8.	Processing must be progressive and continuous.	17.	Machines should be designed to suit the tasks they perform.
9.	A time cycle must be set and maintained.	18.	The system of production must benefit everyone – consumers, workers, and owners.

understood and appreciated by all those who contemplate the setting up a flow-line system."

Woollard quickly shifted from principles that were "virtually axiomatic" to axioms. What is the difference between a principle and an axiom? These terms are defined as follows [4]:

Principle	A basic truth, law, or assumption.
Axiom	A self-evident or universally recognized truth.

The difference between a principle and an axiom is that an axiom is self-evident while a principle may not be (hence, "virtually axiomatic"). A principle is a less rigorous term for a true statement, while an axiom is a more formal description of a true statement that requires no proof. In addition, a set of axioms must be self-consistent and not lead to conclusions that contradict one another. So why did Woollard, towards the end of his life, believe his 18 principles were in fact 18 axioms?

Woollard's extensive experience with flow production beginning in 1904 taught him that every one of the 18 axioms was necessary in order to achieve flow production. However, are these axioms really self-evident and require no proof? Readers who are familiar with flow production will recognize that each one of the 18 axioms must be in place for flow production to exist.

But would people not familiar with flow production recognize these as self-evident and requiring no proof? No, they would not. If they did, then flow would be commonplace. Batch-and-queue processing would not exist, push scheduling software systems (MRP) would never have been created, and there would have been no need to establish organizations whose sole purpose is to train people in Lean management.

The 18 principles are axioms, self-evident and not requiring any proof, only among those who have actually achieved flow; specifically, those who have built flow-lines first-hand. This constitutes a relatively small number of people because most managers ignore or cherry-pick the axioms they like the most and are thus unable to achieve flow in production (or service) activities.

Woollard's initial characterization of the 18 items as principles is the better description. He did readers a great service by providing the 18 principles and a body of related information to help them introduce flow in their businesses. Woollard's insight was certainly unique for the time, and that is still the case today.

The things that Woollard did in the 1920s to achieve flow, which in today's Lean lexicon are called standardized work, Just-In-Time, supermarkets, autonomation, takt/cycle time, quick change-over, etc., are the things that anyone must do for any product or service at any time in history or in the future to achieve flow. People must discover these innovations by themselves or through the pioneering work of others; there is no way around them. Flow is the common denominator that drives everyone to the same principles and practices. The point of convergence is singular.

Frank Woollard's eighteenth principle of flow production is worth emphasizing because it relates to the great difficulty that most organizations have in establishing the Lean management system. Woollard said (principle 18):

> "The system of production must benefit everyone –
> consumers, workers, and owners."

Woollard recognized that in order for flow to exist, the interests of key stakeholders – and today we would also include suppliers and communities – must not be marginalized (i.e. win-lose). In other words, flow can function only when practiced in a non-zero-sum manner (i.e. win-win). That makes abundant sense. For example, employees who lose their jobs as a result of productivity improvements (win for the company, lose for the employee) will have been harmed by flow and those who survive will refuse, in covert and overt ways, to establish, maintain, and improve the system. Flow must cause no harm.

Flow, which is the most productive and satisfying working condition, cannot exist when senior managers are committed to a zero-sum mindset. Unfortunately, most executives cannot envision anything other than zero-sum outcomes. This intellectual handicap – one of many when it comes to understanding Lean management – causes enterprise-wide queuing which, of course, makes flow impossible.

Notes

[1] F.G. Woollard, *Principles of Mass and Flow Production*, Iliffe & Sons, Ltd., London, U.K., 1954. Woollard's book was published for distribution in the United States one year later by Philosophical Library, New York, NY. The exact reference is: F.G. Woollard, *Principles of Mass and Flow Production*, Philosophical Library Inc., New York, NY, 1955

[2] F.G. Woollard with B. Emiliani, *Principles of Mass and Flow Production*, 55th Anniversary Special Reprint Edition, The CLBM, LLC, Wethersfield, Conn., 2009

[3] F.G. Woollard, *Flow Production and Automation: Eighteen Axioms*, Industrial Administration Group, College of Technology Birmingham (now Aston Business School, Aston University, Birmingham), U.K., 1954, with Foreword by Professor David Bramley, Department of Industrial Administration, College of Technology (22 pp)

[4] *The American Heritage College Dictionary*, Third Edition, Houghton, New York, NY, 1998, p. 97 and 1088

[5] See B. Emiliani, *REAL LEAN: The Keys to Sustaining Lean Management*, Volume Three, The CLBM, LLC, Wethersfield, Conn., 2008

Toyota's British Influence

Unaware of the details of Toyota's history, it's easy to think that Toyota managers and workers were the originators of all the important ideas. In fact, they were the originators of some important ideas and adopters of ideas from many others[†]– most good, but a few not so good. This article highlights one idea that originated in the U.K. and which Toyota senior managers have for decades found very useful for determining the size and output of their automobile plants, and for informing them when to develop new models.

For many years I have been interested in the origins and evolution of Lean management and have recently written book chapters and papers on the topic [1-4]. During the course of my studies I have periodically come across references made by Toyota executives and others to the Maxcy-Silberston production cost curve, invariably without attribution or with erroneous attribution. As a result, the original source for the curve had long been difficult to locate.

The curve appeared in the 1959 book *The Motor Industry*, a landmark study of the British automotive industry from the early 1900s to 1957, written by economists George Maxcy and Aubrey Silberston [5]. Importantly, the book also included a description of how the cost curve was derived [6], which I will discuss later. Figure 1 shows the elusive Maxcy-Silberston cost curve (also known as an "experience curve").

This curve describes a quasi-empirical relationship between the total cost per unit and annual production volume for a hypothetical "unit" consisting of a mix of different models of

Figure 1

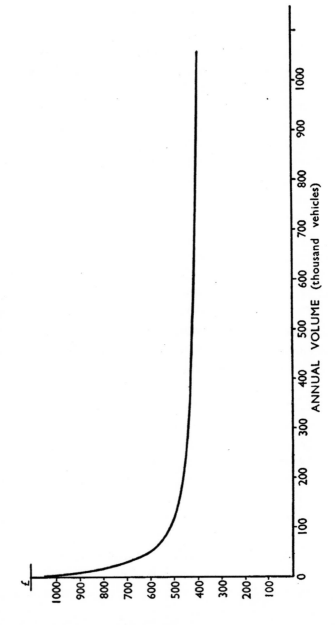

mass-market cars, vans, and trucks, "with varying degrees of interchangeability between them," in the U.K. in the early- to mid-1950s (a high growth period). The shape of the curve suggests there is little in the way of economies of scale beyond a cumulative output of about 200,000 to 250,000 units per year.

Since the late 1950s, Toyota senior executives have viewed this cost curve as helpful in guiding their thinking and decision-making with respect to the size and output of new automobile plants [7]. Taiichi Ohno accepted the Maxcy-Silberston cost curve for 15 years during Toyota's high-growth (sellers' market) period, from about 1958 to 1973. The Maxcy-Silberston cost curve loses relevance in slow growth (buyers' market) periods, such as what Toyota started to experience after the 1973 oil shock, according to Ohno [8]. While Ohno thought that Toyota's Production System invalidated or greatly undercut economy of scale effects and the Maxcy-Silberston cost curve, the Maxcy-Silberston curve seems to still be relevant to Toyota senior management's thinking in terms of annual factory production output. The question is, why?

In 1994 when I was a manufacturing manager at Pratt & Whitney, I can vividly recall our kaizens and the hundreds of wonderful improvements that we made to our products and processes. We were achieving for the first time quick set-ups, short or no queue times, tremendous reductions in part travel, improvements in quality, etc. These kaizens, many of which were facilitated by sensei Doi Yoshihisa, then of Shingijutsu Co., Ltd., were practical and helped our business unit tremendously.

I can also vividly recall meeting with finance executives each month who would project onto the screen a production cost curve of an earlier product, onto which was superimposed an anticipated production cost curve for the new product we were producing. I was struck by the enormous disconnect in how operations people went about reducing cost, through fundamental process improvement, compared to how finance managers viewed cost reduction, theoretically through economies of scale and production cost curves. Their task, unlike Mr. Doi's task, was to drive us to hit points on a simplistic, arbitrarily-determined cost curve. The dissonance was jarring and unforgettable.

In 1999 sensei Doi came to Hartford, Connecticut, from Yokohama, Japan, to facilitate kaizens at local first-tier aerospace suppliers. Production cost curves were still on my mind five years later, and so I asked him at dinner one night what he thought of the relationship between cost and production volume. I asked Mr. Doi this question in part because it was conspicuously absent from the early Lean production and Lean accounting literature [9] and I thought he might know why.

Almost before I could finish asking the question, sensei sternly admonished me – actually rapping me on the head with his knuckles – telling me that it was not the right way to think. Instead, Mr. Doi said people must think this way: If a manufacturer expects to meet customers' expectations with respect to prices in competitive markets, then costs must decline as a function of time, not volume, by improving designs and processes from beginning to end. He drew a sketch on the placemat to explain what he meant and it made perfect sense, but I still had questions.

For many years I had viewed the type of cost-volume relationship expressed in the Maxcy-Silberston curve as fundamentally flawed because it promotes overproduction under any market condition. However, I remained curious as to why this relationship was conspicuously absent from the Lean literature written by Japanese authors in the 1980s and 1990s – it was not even directly refuted until the onset of the post-1973 slow-growth period cited by Ohno [8]. It was as if the cost-volume relationship was such an obviously stupid way to think that it was not even worth mentioning in any of the most important books. Yet it shaped the thinking of Toyota executives for decades, and apparently successfully so. Again, the question is why?

The Maxcy-Silberston production cost curve keeps popping up, most recently in the 2006 book, *Inside the Mind of Toyota*, by Satoshi Hino [10], and in Masaaki Sato's 2008 book *The Toyota Leaders* [11]. Hino says that the Maxcy-Silberston cost curve is still relevant to Toyota management after almost 50 years. He says that the value of the curve to Toyota senior managers is different. To most executives, the cost curve says they should seek to increase the annual production volume of a factory from 200,000 to 1,000,000 units to maximize economies of scale and achieve the lowest possible production costs. To Toyota mangers, the curve suggested something different: that "...it would be more profitable to increase overall sales by developing new models..." [12].

From Toyota's viewpoint, producing more than 250,000 vehicles was ill-advised because there was little additional cost savings to be had from economy of scale effects. So instead of focusing on securing the last drop of cost savings, they should determine what other products customers want and manufacture new models that satisfy those needs. This unique view of the Maxcy-Silberston cost curve helped Toyota become a full-line automaker and grow to become the industry leader in 2008.

The cost curve was originally created by Maxcy and Silberston to provide guidance to British auto industry executives, which at that time consisted of five major companies: British Motor Corporation (formed in a 1952 merger of Morris Motors Ltd. and Austin Motor Company, Ltd.), Ford, Rootes, Standard, and Vauxhall. Its purpose was to give the executives an estimate of the expected reductions in cost per unit that could be achieved if annual production volumes were increased. This information provided an indication of the future growth potential at the level of the firm and of the industry as a whole.

In the late-1940s through the mid-1950s, each British motor company produced 50,000 to 200,000 vehicles per year, where the volume of popular models ranged from 50,000 to 100,000 per year. The Maxcy-Silberston automobile production cost curve showed that doubling or tripling production volume would yield large cost savings. The British motor industry thus had considerable room for growth, according to the economists, as sales would surely grow as costs and prices fell.

The economists were telling British auto executives that growth, and therefore future success (and survival), is best achieved by becoming more supply-driven; to overproduce. That is, they should become more aggressively supply-driven (e.g. 30% supply-driven, 70% demand-driven) where a larger supply of vehicles at lower prices will create greater demand, versus relying on customer demand for vehicles at current prices to create the necessary supply (e.g. 10% supply-driven, 90% demand-driven) – which is what the British motor industry had largely done for much of its early existence. Expanding the supply of existing vehicles and creating new vehicles, however, consumes financial and other resources necessary for improving auto parts, creating new automotive technologies, and updating established products to help ensure long-term survival. So there is risk in being supply-driven, and it is not solely related to the cost of new products and expanded inventories.

The Maxcy-Silberston cost curve graphically supports the argument for automakers to focus more on economies of scale and become more supply-driven (and also becoming more cost focused and financially-driven). However, the data used to generate the curve was based on two flimsy pieces of information: "the small amount of available [published] quantitative evidence" and estimates from one major U.K. automobile company "based solely on an opinion" [13]. The major U.K. automobile company from which the opinion came was a subsidiary of a U.S. automaker [14].

It is astonishing that Toyota executives would put so much faith in the Maxcy-Silberston cost curve given: 1) how it was derived; 2) the fact that it was a rough estimate, a simple model used to describe complex inter-connected relationships; and 3) that it was rooted in batch-and-queue processing and standard cost accounting [15]. Note how the neatly drawn continuous line in Figure 1 deceptively suggests rigorous research and precise data [16].

The Maxcy-Silberston cost curve informed Toyota executives on many big business decisions, each costing hundreds of millions of dollars. Apparently Toyota's own standard cost accounting data post-1965 validated the Maxcy-Silberston cost curve sufficiently well to warrant its continued use even as growth slowed after 1973. In addition, Toyota's unique interpretation of the curve has apparently served it well for several decades [17] compared to competitors who unwisely sought to produce larger and larger volumes as the principal means to reduce costs. This expansion of volume and associated investments proved to be a mistake once consumer markets began to diversify, competition increased, and growth slowed.

While in Ohno's view the Toyota Production System eliminates the need for scale [8], other Toyota senior executives, one after another, apparently saw a need for scale to drive down costs [18]. However, the flaw that is built into the Maxcy-Silberston cost curve is that it compels company executives to authorize producing too many of one product, to produce too many different products, or to do both, resulting in gluts of supply, especially in contracting markets.

Management commitment to the Maxcy-Silberston cost curve eventually leads to a systemic breakdown of discipline needed to fulfill actual customer demand at the required price [19]. It seems that however the Maxcy-Silberston cost curve is interpreted, it will outlive its usefulness sooner or later and cause a lot of trouble. Therefore, it is not a valid model for executive decision-making, even if the data were rigorous and precise [15, 20]. Toyota finally fell victim to the Maxcy-Silberston cost curve in 2008, having experienced less severe problems with it in the late-1980s and early-1990s [21].

So what now? It would not make sense for Toyota to continue to pursue a dubious representation of economies of scale (Figure 1), even when economic conditions improve, because it would only lead to a repetition of errors. What Toyota (and others) can do is de-emphasize economies of scale thinking and totally eliminate the use of production cost curves. A return to its long-standing policy of stable long-term growth (3-5% per year), from which it deviated between 1998-2008, would be helpful, as would supplying to actual customer demand. The way to do that is to focus on achieving flow [22] as Frank Woollard did in the 1920s [4] and Taiichi Ohno [8] did in 1970s. (Note that achieving flow in sellers' markets improves gross profit margins, so the rationale for pursuing flow transcends any specific market condition).

Figure 2 shows why achieving flow is so important: it removes the deep bend at the start of the Maxcy-Silberston cost curve [15]. The decline in cost in the Woollard-Ohno curve is due to a huge reduction in time – principally set-up time, queue time, and transportation time – not an increase in volume. The positive impact on both profitability and competitiveness is obvious.

Figure 2

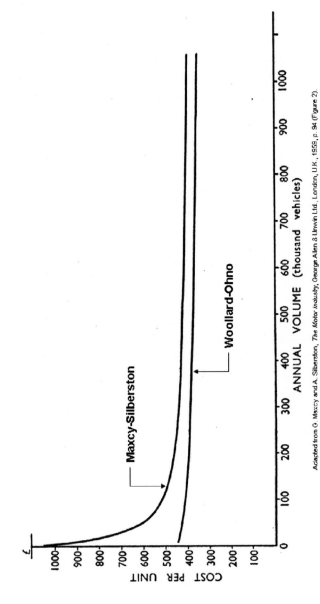

Adapted from G. Maxcy and A. Silberston, *The Motor Industry*, George Allen & Unwin Ltd., London, U.K., 1959, p. 94 (Figure 2).

Notes

† One of Toyota's great accomplishments has been in putting these ideas together to create a beautifully integrated management system, steadily improving it day-by-day, and then maintaining commitment to the system through generations of managers. However, it is clear they have stumbled badly in recent years. Their self-imposed high growth period from 1998-2008 seems to be the key factor that has led to numerous problems that will be difficult to correct.

[1] M.L. Emiliani, "The Origins of Lean Management in America: The Role of Connecticut Businesses," *Journal of Management History*, Vol. 12, No. 2, 2006, pp. 167-184

[2] B. Emiliani, *REAL LEAN: Critical Issues and Opportunities in Lean Management*, Volume Two, The CLBM, LLC, Wethersfield, Conn., 2007, Chapters 1-4 and 10

[3] B. Emiliani, *REAL LEAN: The Keys to Sustaining Lean Management*, Volume Three, The CLBM, LLC, Wethersfield, Conn., 2008

[4] F. Woollard with B. Emiliani, *Principles of Mass and Flow Production*, The CLBM, LLC, Wethersfield, Conn., 2009

[5] G. Maxcy and A. Silberston, *The Motor Industry*, George Allen & Unwin Ltd., London, U.K., 1959, p. 94 (Figure 2). Used with permission. The shape of the curve is approximately that of a 90% experience curve, which means there is a 10% reduction in cost each time cumulative production volume is doubled. This is the book that led me (Emiliani) to Frank G. Woollard's long-forgotten work in flow production in the 1920s British automotive industry. See note [4].

[6] Maxcy and Silberston, pp. 86-93 and 98

[7] The book *Toyota: A History of the First 50 Years* (Toyota Motor Corporation, Toyota City, Japan, 1988), lists on page 506 under the heading "General Studies" a reference to G. Maxcy and A. Silberston's book *The Motor Industry*. This book was important enough to Toyota executives to be listed in the company's official history.

[8] T. Ohno, *Toyota Production System*, Productivity Press, Portland, OR, 1988, pp. 1-2. The original subtitle to Ohno's 1978 book *The Toyota Production System* (published in Japanese by Diamond Inc., Tokyo, Japan) was "Aiming to Manage Free from Economies of Scale" (see Jon Miller's explanations of the subtitle at http://www.gembapantarei.com/2007/06/10_common_misconceptions_about.html and

http://www.gembapantarei.com/2009/01/the_toyota_production_system_b

y_taiichi_ohno_chapt.html). Ohno thought Toyota's production system invalidated or greatly undercut economy of scale thinking and the Maxcy-Silberston cost curve due to the dramatic reduction in set-up time, queue time, transportation time, etc., as a result of achieving flow.

[9] See Yasuhiro Monden's books on operations and cost management in the Japanese automotive industry, for example.

[10] S. Hino, *Inside the Mind of Toyota*, Productivity Press, New York, NY, 2006, pp. 80-82

[11] M. Sato, *The Toyota Leaders*, Vertical Inc., New York, NY, 2008, p. 148

[12] Hino, pp. 80-82

[13] Maxcy and Silberston, p. 88

[14] Personal communication with Aubrey Silberston, at the Oxford and Cambridge Club, London, UK, 19 May 2009

[15] The empirical studies conducted by The Boston Consulting Group in the mid-1960s to validate the experience curve are flawed because they reflect nothing more than the widespread practice of batch-and-queue processing and standard cost accounting (and under the narrow conditions that they examined, where product or industry growth rates were very high and prices were set by management; i.e. sellers' market, price = cost + profit). See *Perspectives on Experience*, The Boston Consulting Group, Inc., Boston, MA, 1972. Confusion has arisen because the human experience of learning a new task can produce a similarly shaped curve. The Maxcy-Silberston automobile production cost curve and The Boston Consulting Group's misnamed experience curve are identical, and both are independent of the growth rate of the firm or industry. The proper name for these would be the "scale cost curve," as distinct from the "human experience curve." The reason why Ohno viewed a firm's growth rate as relevant to the Maxcy-Silberston automobile production cost curve is as follows: High growth amortizes waste, unevenness, and unreasonableness rapidly over a large volume of goods produced in a short period of time at prices set by the manufacturer (i.e. sellers' market), which customers are willing to pay. When conditions reverse and a buyers' market emerges, customers are no longer willing to pay the prices set by manufacturers, nor are they willing to pay for activities that add cost but do not add value. Therefore, Toyota's production (and overall management) system, which seeks to eliminate waste, unevenness, and unreasonableness, undercuts the need for scale that would otherwise be necessary to enable a manufacturer to produce goods at low cost. In other words, the need for scale in operations diminishes as the amount of waste, unevenness, and unreasonableness diminish and flow improves (see Figure 2). Frank G. Woollard recognized this effect when he

established flow production at Morris Motors Ltd. (like Toyota, in vertically disintegrated production – which is very different than the vertically integrated Ford Model T production at Highland Park) in the mid-1920s (see note [4]).

[16] In his 1960 review of the book *The Motor Industry*, John B. Rae wrote that "...[the author's] work is excellent; their book can be rated as indispensable." In the chapter analyzing the economies of mass production (Chapter 6, pp. 75-98), Professor Rae said: "...[the chapter] is done with a thoroughness that has not to my knowledge been applied to the American automobile industry." This illustrates how even skilled book reviewers can miss important details. See J.B. Rae, "Book review of *The Motor Industry* by G. Maxcy and A. Silberston," *The Economic History Review*, Vol. 13, No. 1, 1960, pp. 132-133.

[17] It appears Toyota continues to use the Maxcy-Silberston automobile production cost curve – created in the era of mechanical vehicles powered by internal combustion engines made using 1950s production technology – in this new era of electro-mechanical vehicles powered by gas-electric hybrid, electric, and hydrogen systems made using contemporary production technologies.

[18] This view may be driven by the capital intensive nature of automobile production and the widespread use of standard cost accounting.

[19] Success breeds complacency, and what better measure of success is there than higher sales?

[20] To understand the madness that can occur when top executives become fully possessed by the spell of economies of scale thinking, you must read "The Mega Containers Invade," John W. Miller, *The Wall Street Journal*, 26 January 2009. This is one example of what I call a "durable" error. It is the type of error in management thinking that survives for decades through generations of managers.

[21] T. Fujimoto, *The Evolution of a Manufacturing System at Toyota*, Oxford University Press, New York, NY, 1999, pp. 206-222

[22] Achieve flow not just in production, but in all activities in the enterprise, in a non-zero-sum fashion, consistent with the "Respect for People" principle.

[23] In a 1972 paper, Aubrey Silberston provided a detailed technical analysis of economies of scale ("savings of resources associated with large scale"). His analysis vividly illustrates an enormous disconnect between how economists understand economies of scale compared to the simplistic manner in which executives comprehend and seek economies of scale.

Unfortunately, the paper is also rich with so many qualifications, and misses key factors which can lead to diseconomies of scale (the inability to save resources), that it renders the economies of scale argument as practically useless – details which executives are typically unaware of. Also, Silberston erroneously thought that all economies contributed to scale or were scalable. See A. Silberston, "Economies of Scale in Theory and Practice," *The Economic Journal*, Vol. 82, No. 325, March 1972, pp. 369-391.

[24] Eiji Toyoda, the former chairman of Toyota Motor Corporation, was a principal advocate of the Maxcy-Silberston production cost curve. Despite his enthusiasm for the curve, Mr. Toyoda seemed to be aware that it could suggest to senior managers that they authorize production of many different products. In a 1998 interview of Eiji Toyoda, Takahiro Fujimoto asked the question: "What was your rule of thumb for deciding when to build a new plant? Did you have an upper limit in mind for production volume at each plant?" Mr. Toyoda's answer is as follows: "...our basic unit of production capacity is about 20,000 vehicles per month... Twenty thousand seems to be some sort of natural economic unit... *you can only sell 20,000 vehicles a month with each model if you have just a few models*" [italics added]. In other words, an automaker must not produce too many models; if it does, then it cannot reach the "natural economic unit" of 20,000 vehicles per month in production. Apparently Toyota senior managers did not share Eiji Toyoda's concern and thus produced too many models and created too much production capacity between approximately 1998 and 2008. Source: *The Birth of Lean*, K. Shimokawa and T. Fujimoto, editors, The Lean Enterprise Institute, Cambridge, MA, 2009, p. 252. This book, *The Birth of Lean*, is improperly titled because the birth of Lean pre-dates Toyota Motor Corporation. The book should have instead been titled: *The Birth of Toyota's Production System*.

[25] Sato, pp. 132-133.

[26] One of Toyota's long-standing strengths has been to gather intelligence from many sources – competitors, suppliers, customers, analysts, academics, etc. – carefully evaluate this information, and then put it to practical use. Their study of books such as *The Motor Industry* and competitor's products and production systems helped them become who they are today. The question is, will information such as the Maxcy-Silberston cost curve still be considered useful in the future?

A Message From the Future

The year is 2060. The changes that have taken place in business over the last 50 years have been many and varied, and mostly for the better. Advances in corporate information technology are astonishing compared to 2030. Yet despite many advances, some management practices have undergone relatively little change. In the 250 or so years since enterprises came under more-or-less thoughtful management, some facets of management have stubbornly resisted additional improvement.

For example, there remains a tendency among leaders to treat their stakeholders poorly at times. Also, there is still a surprising absence of flow in information and work activities, from executive offices down to the factory or office floor, and generally between stakeholders, despite the great advances in information technologies. It appears that the management system in use today remains somewhat inadequate relative to the needs of people, which technology cannot remedy.

It has been 180 years since the birth of Lean management, beginning with Frederick Taylor's Scientific Management in the 1880s, which also marks the start of modern industrial engineering. Over this period of time there have been only two serous challengers to conventional management: Scientific Management (1880-1940) and Lean management (1975-2030). Both failed as alternative management systems, but they did succeed in adding many new buzzwords and tools to managers' toolkits. Many of these tools remain in use today, but mostly within the framework of conventional management, which of course is devoid of flow.

Lean management has been all but dead since about 2030. It survives in a small number of small- and mid-size companies and only a few large global corporations, not surprisingly, Toyota Motor Corporation and Honda. Toyota started to lose their way around 1998. It began to recover in 2010, but overall managers and employees struggled to keep Lean management going. That proved there is no such thing as Lean DNA. For some reason it has been less difficult for Honda, who is now the world leader in both personal mobility products and robotic assistance systems for the elderly and people with physical disabilities.

Toyota's grand stumble in 2008-2009 gave an enormous supply of ammunition to the critics of Lean management. They ridiculed the "triumph of Lean" and began characterizing Lean as a myth. Toyota's come-down provided the evidence that legions of status-quo oriented managers needed so they could ignore Lean. Lean became "your father's Oldsmobile," as that old saying goes. Generation Y did not have much interest in Lean management because so many had seen their parents negatively impacted personally and professionally by botched Lean implementations.

Every organization devoted to advancing Lean management went the way of the Taylor Society and closed their doors due to declining interest. Unfortunately, the most knowledgeable and skilled Lean practitioners, consultants, trainers, and educators worked independently from one another for decades and thus failed to capitalize on their strengths. They did not work together as a team to achieve their shared objectives and to better serve customers. The Lean movement faded as the key figures retired or passed away.

The Great Recession of 2007-2009 did not prove to be as beneficial to Lean management as many had anticipated. Instead of being a once in a lifetime "burning platform," as they used to say, to initiate change, the deep recession caused most executives to stick with the devil they know: conventional management. Lean required too much delicate thinking and hard learning for which executives had no time.

Managers were in survival mode and had lost all desire to create new corporate cultures. The use of Lean tools surged, a bubble so to speak, as a means to achieve short-term cost reduction to survive the Great Recession. Manager's interest was in quick, 90-day payoffs using Lean tools, just as Lean leaders began to strongly advocate moving away from Lean tools to Lean management. The use of Lean tools became even more deeply embedded in management practice, even when the economy improved. This further damaged Lean management's credibility.

Managers cut millions of jobs during the Great Recession and then used Lean tools to improve productivity and avoid hiring new workers. The stagnant economy and burdens of sustained unemployment and healthcare costs on society grew great, and so managers turned their attention to innovation, design thinking, and entrepreneurship to develop so-called "game changing" products and services. Fundamental process improvement and culture change was seen by executives as too slow and yielding little or no fruit in comparison to the value that had to be created quickly to pay for growing social needs. And since accounting systems did not materially improve from that developed in the early 1900s, managers continued to view economies of scale (increased sales volumes) as the principal means to reduce unit costs in production.

For the first 30 years of its existence, roughly 1975-2005, the Lean community failed to understand Lean management, seeing it as tools to improve efficiency and productivity in operations. By the time they began to understand Lean as a management system, and also recognize the importance of the "Respect for People" principle and what it meant, it was too late. The Lean community almost exactly followed the path taken by the leaders of Scientific Management movement between 1910-1940 and repeated most of their errors.

Despite not having worked out as desired, both Scientific Management and Lean management led to some important improvements in business practices, productivity, and performance. Some improvement, the result of "90-day Lean," is better than no improvement, you could say. They wanted all the benefits without any of the commitment. What a mistake it was to endorse Lean lite and validate taking shortcuts to achieve momentary prosperity. Managers should have done much more because people's lives, to a great extent, depended upon achieving better outcomes.

With Lean management now at its nadir, the time is again right for some daring and thoughtful people to understand why and how Scientific Management and Lean management failed to displace conventional management and start anew. It may turn out that the third time is the charm. The two earlier tries were probably destined to largely fail in part because supporters for too long lacked awareness of Lean principles, their relation to the tools, the intent of Scientific Management and Lean management (stable long-term growth, not cost-cutting), or the problems that they would encounter.

So how can someone go about resurrecting Lean management? What would have to be done to assure broader success in the third iteration, rather than a few isolated examples that struggled to sustain themselves over time in the second iteration? They would certainly have to do a lot of root cause analysis, and will surely have to take the following actions:

- The name "Lean" management is a problem and must be changed. Call it "progressive management" instead. After all, that is fundamentally what Scientific Management and Lean management represent – a positive progression away from conventional management. The term "Lean" was always disliked by its advocates because it so strongly implied negative attributes such as thinning, cutting, inadequate resources, and laying people off. So, the name has to change.

- Progressive management will be presented as a comprehensive management system from the outset, never as a set of tools, and never used as a tactic to speed people up.

- The leaders of the third progressive management movement (3PM) should be very well-versed in the history of Scientific Management and Lean management. They will understand the paths previously taken, the successes, and the root causes of mistakes that were made so they do not repeat unfavorable outcomes.

- Progressive management's principles, "Continuous

Improvement" and "Respect for People," will be at the forefront from the very beginning. Tools will be presented as subservient to the principles, and the tools will be used in part to achieve the "Respect for People" principle.

- The advocates of progressive management will develop and propagate uniform messages consistently over time. They will use one definition of progressive management that incorporates several key elements: The win-win nature of progressive management; the fact the it is principle-based (where "Continuous Improvement" and "Respect for People" are timeless); the management system is focused on creating value for end-use customers; there is an intent to compete on the basis of time and achieve flow, helped by the elimination of waste, unevenness, and unreasonableness; and that the scientific method is the approach used to understand and correct problems. A single, well-written definition will alleviate discontent among executives who in the past were very confused by shifting definitions and incorrect interpretations of Lean management.

- The universal truths of flow will be made explicit. That anyone wanting to achieve material and information flow, which is the goal of progressive management, must learn or discover for themselves the requirement in all cases for just-in-time, kanban, quick change-over, visual controls, mistake-proofing, takt time, production leveling, etc., to use the old terminology.

- The human, economic, political, and legal benefits of progressive management are expansive and will be made very clear to all stakeholders, and especially to corporate leaders, the media, and students in colleges and universities. Operational aspects of progressive management, which was its focus between 1975-2007 and proved to be not a strength but a major weakness, will no longer be of primary importance. The new focus will be the application of progressive management for the enterprise and the extended enterprise.

- Recognize the good work that was done by prior progressive management practitioners, consultants, trainers, and educators. Their work and perspectives should be incorporated into the new progressive management system, thereby presenting a more comprehensive management system than was the case in previous eras. They include (in alphabetical order): Charles Allen; Carl Barth; Art Byrne; Morris Cooke; Training Within Industry leaders Channing Dooley, Walter Dietz, Mike Kane, and Bill Conover; Bob Emiliani; Henry Ford; Takahiro Fujimoto; Henry Gantt; Frank and Lillian Gilbreth; Yoshiki Iwata; Daniel Jones; George Koenigsaecker; Jeffrey Liker; Brian Maskell; Yasuhiro Monden; Taiichi Ohno; Harlow Person; Charles Sorensen; Frederick Taylor; Eiji Toyoda; Peter Ward; James Womack; Frank Woollard; and so on.

- The advocates of progressive management will work together and they will not succumb to individual or organizational politics. This will be seen as inconsis-

with progressive management's principles and as
 te that hinders their abilities to achieve shared
_ _ectives and to better serve customers.

- A knowledge database will be created and available on-demand to progressive management practitioners via smartphones, to help keep them tightly on course. It will provide some answers on-demand, but will also promote practitioners' efforts to think through their own specific problems using progressive management principles and practices.

- Broad-based efforts will be made to discourage current and future executives from cherry-picking Lean management and reducing it to a bunch of tools. The progressive management knowledge database can help with this.

- Exploitative consultants will remain a major threat to progressive management because they will do what they always do: cherry-pick the tools and sell them to executives as cost-cutting programs for quick hits to the bottom line. Efforts will have to be made to limit their attractiveness and isolate the damage that they cause.

Whoever resurrects progressive management will have to do these things at minimum, and likely much more, if they wish to have anything more than the relatively small impact generated by their predecessors. The key to success will be to study and learn the lessons from both Scientific Management and Lean management. Their histories will shape future success.

2 Learn From Others

Our attention is captivated by successful companies while we rush to ignore those that have made big mistakes or who have failed. However, failure is a much more substantive source for learning than success. Today's bridge design, construction, and maintenance, for example, are the results of detailed study of yesterday's many bridge failures. Engineers improve products by studying how earlier versions fail. However, managers rarely think to improve their understanding and practice of Lean management by studying how others have failed. That needs to change.

Since 2004 I have taught a unique graduate-level course that carefully analyzes the mistakes and failures of conventionally managed and Fake Lean businesses. The key learning from that course is that the mistakes made are remarkably similar, while the people, product or service, company, industry, time, or place are different. In some cases, the same mistakes are repeated by the same company, sometimes under the same leadership and other times under different leadership. The decision-making traps and flawed theories and assumptions that managers operate under are amazingly similar and illustrate the extent to which most executives accept conventional wisdom and have given up questioning things.

Start studying the failures of companies, including those who have gone down the path of Lean management. Pay very close attention to cause-and-effect and question everything. Create A3 reports of the problems, document the flawed assumptions and the metrics used, and share this information with other managers. Doing so will help ensure your own personal and company success.

The Toyota Half-Way

Just about everyone interested in Lean management has by now heard of The Toyota Way. But have you ever heard of The Toyota Half-Way? Probably not, but that is exactly what most people are doing in their Lean activities.

In April 2001, Toyota Motor Corporation produced a document for internal use called "The Toyota Way 2001" [1]. It is a 13-page booklet, produced at the request of the then-president Fujio Cho, that describes the unique aspects of Toyota's culture that contributed to its success. The document was produced to help ensure a consistent understanding of The Toyota Way among all associates in response to the rapid growth and globalization of Toyota Motor Corporation.

However, as Mr. Kazuhara, the general manager of final assembly at Toyota's Motomachi plant, told me on 14 June 2001, the fact that The Toyota Way has been written down means nothing: "Words are just words, there is more to it [the Toyota Way] than just words." He said it is the responsibility of each supervisor to bring The Toyota Way to life through daily practice and training of future generations of managers and associates on-the-job [2].

There are two pillars of The Toyota Way: "Continuous Improvement" and "Respect for People," as shown in Figure 1 [3]. "Continuous Improvement" consists of three elements: challenge, improvement, and genchi genbutsu (go to the source). "Respect for People" has of two elements: respect and teamwork. These principles and the five elements are deeply rooted in Toyota's history and the Toyoda family's logical and reality-based philosophy of business. These principles, however, are not new and have long been associated with progressive management [4].

Figure 1

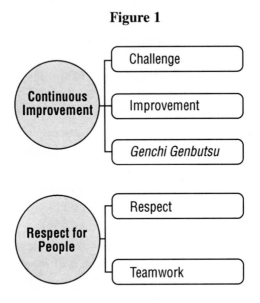

The full extent of publicly available information on The Toyota Way from Toyota Motor Corporation since 2001 is shown in Figure 2 [5]. The two principles and the definitions associated with each of the five elements are just the beginning of much more complete descriptions. It is very important to understand that Toyota does not use a single definition for either of the two principles or for each of the five elements. It uses many definitions and includes real-world examples. Together these create broad descriptions rather than discrete definitions. So please don't go looking for simple definitions where none exist. You have to think for yourself and apply the

"Continuous Improvement" and "Respect for People" principles at work every day to learn what they mean.

Figure 2

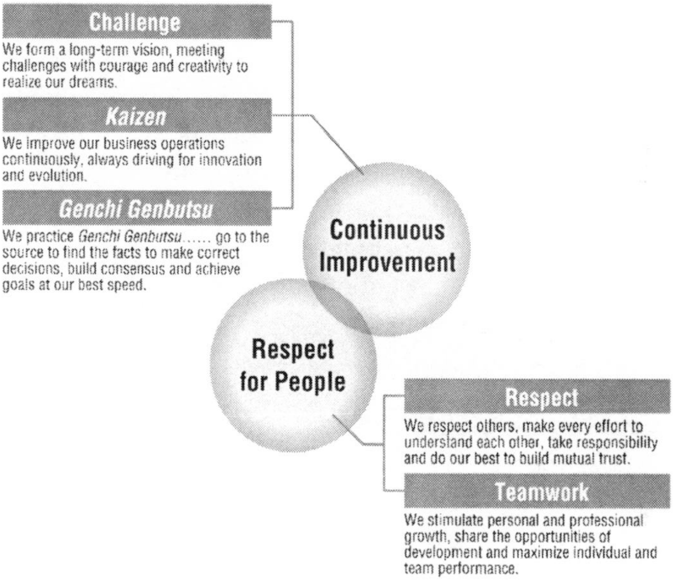

Challenge
We form a long-term vision, meeting challenges with courage and creativity to realize our dreams.

Kaizen
We improve our business operations continuously, always driving for innovation and evolution.

Genchi Genbutsu
We practice *Genchi Genbutsu* ..... go to the source to find the facts to make correct decisions, build consensus and achieve goals at our best speed.

Continuous Improvement

Respect for People

Respect
We respect others, make every effort to understand each other, take responsibility and do our best to build mutual trust.

Teamwork
We stimulate personal and professional growth, share the opportunities of development and maximize individual and team performance.

Today there are numerous books that have the words "The Toyota Way" as the title or subtitle. Surprisingly, all of them focus mostly or exclusively on the "Continuous Improvement" principle. What happened to the "Respect for People" principle? Why is one of the two pillars that are necessary to make Lean management work left out?

The fact that this principle or deep discussion of it, both stand-alone and in relation to the "Continuous Improvement" principle, is missing is not a trivial matter. It is in fact vitally important because throughout the history of progressive management, of which Lean is the current best example, executives have almost always focused solely on continuous improvement – the tools [6] – and ignored the "Respect for People" principle (or its equivalent in earlier times) [7].

If all we do is pay attention to the "Continuous Improvement" principle, then we are in fact following the Toyota Half-Way (Figure 3). Doing so will not yield even half the results. You might get 20% of the benefits if you try really hard.

Figure 3

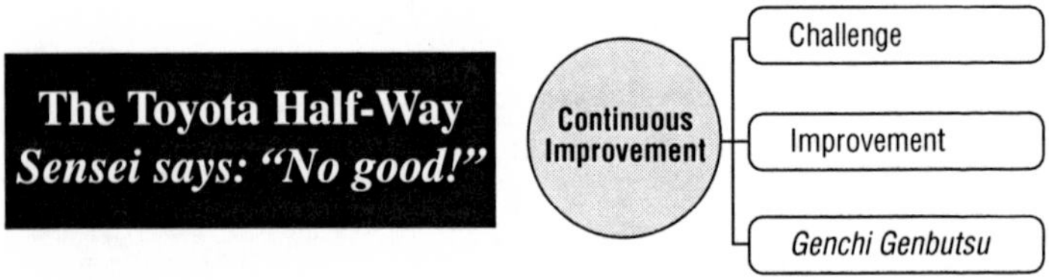

To ignore the "Respect for People" principle is to assure a lot of work and very little actual improvement.

Senior managers always stumble on the "Respect for People" principle because they think this principle is trivial, that they already respect people, or that it can only be put into practice at great cost. Those assumptions are incorrect. For example, if you think shareholders matter more than any other stakeholder, then you do not understand the "Respect for People" principle. If you think purchase price variance and earned hours are good performance metrics, then you do not understand the "Respect for People" principle. If you think that winning at someone else's expense is OK, then you do not understand the "Respect for People" principle. When Lean transformations fail, simple root cause analysis always points to a failure by executives to understand and apply the "Respect for People" principle.

The "Respect for People" principle is understood only through daily practice, on-the-job. It requires years of thought to understand well and can never be completely comprehended. That should be an inspiration, not a deterrent. Along the way, you will realize great results. Now that's a challenge worthy of those who receive big paychecks.

If you are part of a management team, supervisor on up, then it is your responsibility to bring the "Continuous Improvement" and "Respect for People" principles to life by practicing them every day, and to train subordinates so that they in turn can train future generations of managers and associates.

One of Toyota's great accomplishments has been to build upon the work of others before them and add their own important ideas and inventions to create a beautiful, carefully integrated management system, steadily improving it day-by-day, and then maintaining commitment to it through generations of managers [8]. It is a shame to see it cherry-picked time and time again, for the purpose of expediency, and become The Toyota Half-Way in nearly every organization [9].

Please remember that the "Respect for People" principle is not optional. Lean management cannot function properly without it. This principle is everyone's weakness and must now become your focus [10].

Notes

[1] "The Toyota Way 2001," Toyota Motor Corporation, internal document, Toyota City, Japan, April 2001

[2] He also said that once important things are written down they then become unchangeable, and there is a danger in The Toyota Way becoming viewed as unchangeable. The Toyota Way must evolve and adapt over time in response to reality.

[3] "Toyota Environmental and Social Report 2003," Toyota Motor Corporation, Toyota City, Japan, http://www.toyota.co.jp/en/environmental_rep/03/jyugyoin/image15.gif. Image used with permission.

[4] See "The Equally Important Respect for People Principle" by Bob Emiliani, http://www.theclbm.com/respect_for_people.pdf

[5] "Toyota Sustainability Report 2006," Toyota Motor Corporation, Toyota City, Japan, http://www.toyota.co.jp/en/environmental_rep/06/download/pdf/e_report06_p49_p55.pdf. Image used with permission.

[6] Where the tools include: value stream maps, A3 reports, policy deployment, standardized work, 5 Whys, Just-In-Time, visual workplace, set-up reduction, etc.

[7] B. Emiliani, *REAL LEAN: The Keys to Sustaining Lean Management*, Volume Three, The CLBM, LLC, Wethersfield, Conn., 2008, pp. 212-237

[8] However, it is clear Toyota has stumbled badly in recent years. Management's self-imposed high growth period from 1998-2008 seems to be the key factor that has led to numerous problems that will be difficult to correct.

[9] In some departments – such as Finance, Sales, Marketing, Legal, Human Resources, etc. – you will find the "Toyota No-Way," meaning they have zero interest in improving their business process using Lean principles and practices.

[10] This workbook will help you understand the "Respect for People" principle: B. Emiliani, *Practical Lean Leadership: A Strategic Leadership Guide for Executives*, The CLBM, LLC, Wethersfield, Conn., 2008. So will *Better Thinking, Better Results: Case Study and Analysis of an Enterprise-Wide Lean Transformation*, B. Emiliani, with D. Stec, L. Grasso, and J. Stodder, second edition, The CLBM, LLC, Wethersfield, Conn., 2007. This is the first book to describe an enterprise-wide Lean transformation in a real company where both principles of Lean management – "Continuous Improvement" and "Respect for People" – were applied.

Toyota's Dénouement

A combination of self-inflicted wounds more than a decade in the making plus a global economic crisis shows us that Toyota Motor Corporation has lost its way. While not completely unexpected, it is still surprising that Toyota could lose its grasp on key fundamentals of its management system. The company's problems and efforts to recover offer many high-value lessons for any manager who is willing to learn.

For those who study and practice Lean management, Toyota Motor Corporation has always been our guiding star, our true north. But what happens when Toyota turns east, or even south, as they have slowly done over the last decade or so?

Toyota has always been the principal Lean practitioner to learn from because they have done such a brilliant job of putting together a wonderful management system based on work done by other people [1] and through the addition of many of their own unique contributions [2] and steady maintenance and improvement. Their non-zero-sum, principle-based, human-centered management system is undoubtedly the best that has been created in modern times. Its practice should be the norm in any organization, not the exception.

Toyota's recent problems originated with Toyota Global Vision 2010 (launched in 2002 and running through 2010), which, among other things, stated an objective to grow and obtain 15% global market share by the early 2010s. This required Toyota to grow at a compound annual growth rate (CAGR) of nearly 7% per year for a decade (staring from a large base). The owners of this plan and the prior one, Toyota

2003 Vision (launched in 1996 and running through 2005), are the past president and chairman of Toyota, Hiroshi Okuda; the past president and current chairman, Fujio Cho; and the past president and current vice chairman, Katsuaki Watanabe.

Toyota's unraveling came soon after its climax of becoming the world's largest automaker. This outcome shows they, too, are human and make the same mistakes that executives in other companies make: growing too large, too fast. Annual growth of 7% or more is challenging for any organization, big or small, when it is done organically (growth through acquisitions, or a combination of organic growth and acquisitions, can lead to 5- or 10-year CAGRs of 15-30%, which is extremely challenging as well). It is almost double Toyota's CAGR of about 4% in the prior decade.

That begs the question of why did Toyota pursue growth (and profitability) so aggressively? What were its reasons for doing so? Was it to establish a global leadership position in environmental technologies? Was it to obtain a more influential seat at the table in negotiations with governments on auto emissions reduction? Was it to improve the stock price and dividend performance after Toyota became listed on the New York Stock Exchange in 1999? Was it to increase corporate value to avoid a hostile takeover in the rapidly consolidating global auto industry circa 1998? Was it to see if they had the capability to rise to their self-imposed challenge? Or was it simply for the sake of growth itself – to be #1?

Whatever the reasons, I would have expected better judgment and less hubris from Toyota leadership. However, I also realize they are not infallible and will succumb to the same decision-making traps [3] as anyone else. You or I could have made the same mistakes – unless we knew how dangerous high growth can be (see Appendix I – The Growth Imperative).

Having finally recognized the problem fully, Toyota now has a new president, Akio Toyoda, who is leading a back-to-basics approach to designing, selling, and making automobiles. We will all be watching closely in the coming years and decades to see if Toyota can return to its roots of low volume-high variety vehicles (with increasingly diversified power trains) produced using low cost, demand-driven flow production, or if it will eventually become another General Motors (e.g. continuing commitment to a "full product-lineup strategy" [4] with an arrogant sellers' market perspective). This is a major concern for Toyota's new president, Akio Toyoda, who said in June 2009 that "Toyota might well turn into the next GM in a few years" [5]. Let's hope not, but don't bet against it.

So, in what ways did Toyota unravel as a result of its rapid growth? What is the evidence? Here is a summary of Toyota's problems culled from recently published accounts.

- Allowing engineers to put too much expensive content in vehicles [6].
- Making too many large vehicles with low gas mileage and luxury vehicles (i.e. too many models and wrong model line-up for the times) [6, 7].
- Reduction of part commonality within model platforms [8].
- Forgetting how to profitably produce small vehicles [7] and relying on large and luxury vehicles to achieve aggressive sales volume and profit goals [6, 9].

- Stumbling on quality to achieve growth targets [10].
- Not listening to dealers or customers [7]; focusing on the competition instead of customers [6].
- Generally, blocked information flow internally and externally [6], and lacking speed and responsiveness to problems [6, 7].
- Straying from Taiichi Ohno's buyers' market formula of selling price - cost = profit and instead transitioning to the sellers' market formula of selling price = cost + profit [6, 11], resulting in cars incorrectly priced for their market [4, 6]. Basically, adopting the Lexus pricing model to Toyota's mass-market cars.
- Producing to the company's plan rather than producing to dealer and end-use customer demand [9].
- Reduced internal cooperation between sales and manufacturing resulting in over 100 days of unsold inventory (a reduction in global inventory turns from 12 to 3 from mid-2008 through mid-2009) [9].
- Internal blame-game among Toyota executives in the United States and Japan [6, 12].
- Slow to recognize and respond to reality [6, 13]; e.g. change in market and demand from small cars in China [4].
- Installing expensive manufacturing processes [6, 14], building expensive capacity [6], and then suffering from idle capacity (30%) [6, 11]. Generally, succumbing to economies of scale and becoming volume-driven [15, 16, 17].
- Losing focus on manufacturing – the shop floor, the gemba [11, 18].
- Betting on a winning model (the 2010 Prius) to help save the day [7, 10].
- Toyota falls below Honda in Planning Perspective Inc.'s 2009 supplier working relationship index survey [19], caused by increased emphasis on pressuring suppliers to

reduce prices instead of working together to reduce costs.

Wow! It took a global economic crisis to reveal the extent to which Toyota strayed from its roots – and stray it did. From many different directions and for many different reasons, each of the items listed above are inconsistent with The Toyota Way principles of "Continuous Improvement" and "Respect for People" [20].

The critics of Toyota and of Lean management have fully-loaded quivers from which to shoot arrows. This is not a favorable development in terms of our efforts to advance Lean management. In fact, it could turn out to be a major setback. Nevertheless, this is our reality, which we must accept and formulate fact-based responses that acknowledge common imperfections in executive decision-making and honest efforts to recover and improve [21]. Nobody is perfect, not even Toyota senior managers.

The Lean community can lament Toyota's mis-steps or it can learn from them. The latter is much more valuable, of course, and includes the following:

- Years of practice in Lean management does not inoculate individuals or groups of executives from making bad, expensive decisions.
- Groupthink is a common contagion and can even strike Lean thinkers.
- Growth for the sake of growth is foolish; high growth often leads to distress [22].
- Economies of scale thinking will eventually lead to overcapacity and poor responsiveness to changes in demand.

- The value-creating activities within an enterprise should never be taken for granted.
- It is easy to stop listening to intermediate (i.e. distributors) and end-use customers.
- Generally, the grave perils of serving one's self instead of one's customers.

Perhaps the biggest lesson to learn has to do with the basics. Whenever we think we know the basics we become arrogant and then fail to remember and execute the basics. Nobody is so good at whatever they do that they can forget about the basics.

Notes

[1] F.W. Taylor, *The Principles of Scientific Management*, Harper & Brothers Publishers, New York, NY, 1911; F.B. Gilbreth, *Motion Study: A Method for Increasing the Efficiency of the Workman*, D. Van Nostrand Company, New York, NY, 1911; H. Ford with S. Crowther, *My Life and Work*, Garden City Publishing Company Inc., Garden City, NY, 1922; H. Ford with S. Crowther, *Today and Tomorrow*, Doubleday, Page & Company, New York, NY, 1926; D. Dinero, *Training Within Industry: The Foundation Of Lean*, Productivity Press, New York, NY, 2005 (and see also http://trainingwithinindustry.net); F.G. Woollard, with B. Emiliani, *Principles of Mass and Flow Production*, 55th Anniversary Special Reprint Edition, The CLBM, LLC, Wethersfield, Conn., January 2009.

[2] Y. Monden, *Toyota Production System: Practical Approach to Production Management*, Industrial Engineering and Management Press, Norcross, GA, 1983; T. Ohno, *Toyota Production System*, Productivity Press, Portland, OR, 1988; J. Womack, D. Jones, and D. Roos, *The Machine that Changed the World*, Rawson Associates, New York, NY, 1990; Y. Monden, *Toyota Production System: An Integrated Approach to Just-In-Time*, Engineering and Management Press, Norcross, GA, 1998; T. Fujimoto, *The Evolution of a Manufacturing System at Toyota*, Oxford University Press, Inc., New York, NY, 1999; J. Liker, *The Toyota Way*, McGraw-Hill, New York, NY, 2004; A. Iyer, S. Seshadri, and R. Vasher, *Toyota Supply Chain Management*, McGraw-Hill, New York, NY, 2009

[3] J. Hammond, R. Keeney, and H. Raffia, "The Hidden Traps in Decision Making," *Harvard Business Review*, Vol. 76, No. 5, 1998, pp. 47-58.

[4] "Toyota Falters in Booming China," N. Shirouzu, *The Wall Street Journal*, 8 May 2009

[5] "Industry at Intersection of Green, Cheap," *The Nikkei*, 8 June 2009

[6] "A Scion Drives Toyota Back to Basics," N. Shirouzu and J. Murphy, *The Wall Street Journal*, 24 February 2009

[7] "Toyota Loss is Worse than Expected," I. Rowley, *BusinessWeek*, 8 May 2009

[8] "Toyota Targets Y100bn Cut in Small-Car Production Costs," *The Nikkei*, 7 June 2009

[9] "Toyota Too is Looking to Cut Costs," M. Maynard, *The New York Times*, 13 May 2009

[10] "Toyota Review Reveals Need for More Quality Checks," N. Shirouzu, *The Wall Street Journal*, 11 December 2006

[11] "Incoming Toyota Chief Already Leading Back-to-Basics Reform

Drive," *The Nikkei*, 11 May 2009

[12] "Toyota to Revamp in U.S.," C. Tierney, *The Detroit News*, 8 April 2009

[13] "Toyota Tumbles: Slow Reaction Hammers Auto Giant," P. LeBeau, CNBC.com, 8 May 2009

[14] "As Rivals Catch Up, Toyota CEO Spurs Efficiency Drive," N. Shirouzu, *The Wall Street Journal*, 9 December 2006

[15] "Robust Overseas Expansion Now Haunting Japanese Automakers," *The Nikkei*, 15 January 2009

[16] "GM Collapse Highlights Polarization of Auto Business," *The Nikkei*, 4 June 2009

[17] See "Toyota's British Influence" in Section 1.

[18] "New Toyota CEO Seeks Revival by Returning to Basics," *The Nikkei*, 21 January 2009

[19] "Annual Automotive Supplier Survey: 2002-2009 Working Relations Index," Planning Perspectives Inc., 25 May 2009

[20] "The Toyota Way 2001," Toyota Motor Corporation, internal document, Toyota City, Japan, April 2001

[21] "Toyota Annual Report FY 2009," Katsuaki Watanabe Letter to Shareholders, Toyota Motor Corporation, Toyota City, Japan, June 2009, page 2.

[22] G. Probst and S. Raisch, "Organizational Crisis: The Logic of Failure," *Academy of Management Executive*, Vol. 19, No. 1, 2005, pp. 90-105.

3 See Reality

In order to get really good at something, one has to comprehend reality as it is, not as they would like it to be. If I want to improve my bass guitar playing or my golf game, I have to work on those aspects that I am poor at doing. If I ignore my weaknesses, then I will not make any meaningful improvements in my musical abilities or my golf game. Instead, I will be stuck in neutral and likely backslide.

Genchi genbutsu is Japanese and means "go to the source." The intent of the phrase is to compel managers and others to go see problems with their own eyes to better understand causes and take action to correct problems, instead of hearing about problems second-hand and then specifying flawed fixes from afar. It is one of many practices found in Lean management (e.g. kaizen and visual controls) whose purpose is to get people to see what is actually going on so that improvements can be made.

Success with Lean management requires executives to see things as they really are, not as how they are told to them by obsequious subordinates. Performance-oriented executives should hunger to see reality first-hand, but few actually do, preferring instead to lead from an office far removed from the workplace and its problems. Lean efforts taking place under executives who are not interested in seeing reality are doomed to failure.

Executives must learn to comprehend reality first-hand, no matter how ugly it is or how deeply it impacts their core beliefs about business, management, and leadership.

Lean Mash-Up

If you look closely at the Lean transformation efforts of most companies, you will find one critical error that is often made is the combining of Lean principles and practices with non-Lean principles and practices. The confusion that ensues slows down change, leads to many mistakes that require extensive re-work, and is a primary cause of failed Lean transformations.

Most Lean transformation efforts today are actually far from what you would expect in terms of fidelity to REAL LEAN management principles and practices. People may call what they are doing Lean, but it is instead various corrupted forms of Lean, Fake Lean, caused by a lack of attention to detail among top executives. Executives inadvertently mash-up Lean principles and practices with their long-used conventional management (non-Lean) principles, practices, and metrics [1].

Unfortunately, most executives do not see this glaring problem. In fact, some enthusiastically advocate mash-ups, which is not surprising given their general attitude: "It's results that matter; I don't care how you do it." They view management as an assemblage of tools taken from any and every source, useful as long as it fixes today's problem. They do not distinguish between tools taken from a larger system of management and those that are stand-alone adjuncts to contemporary management practice [2].

Doing this is not without consequence. The mash-up causes confusion and conflicts between directives to eliminate waste and directives to meet top-down metrics rooted in batch-and-queue thinking. This causes delays and rework, and inhibits material and information flows. So despite people's best efforts to become Lean, the mash-up prevents them from making much progress. Predictably, people lose interest in Lean and soon executives are on the lookout for the next new tool to add to their toolkit [3]. Workers then must get trained in the new tool, which leads to flavor-of-the-month syndrome and tool fatigue.

The mash-ups take on various forms and are far-ranging in that they affect business principles, business processes, metrics, and even training.

Business Principles

Lean management has two explicit super ordinate principles: "Continuous Improvement" and "Respect for People," where people include the key business stakeholders: employees, suppliers, customers, investors, and communities. Companies that profess to be "doing Lean" often do not recognize either of these principles. Or, they will recognize the "Continuous Improvement" principle, but practice it poorly, and do not recognize the "Respect for People" principle.

Most companies do not operate with any explicit principles. Instead the principles in use must be deduced from management's decisions. Often, management's decisions favor one stakeholder over another, typically investors, which reveals the fundamental principle they use to manage a business: "Our job is to maximize shareholder value" or, closely related to it, "The purpose of business is to make money." Other implicit or explicit principles can include: "We're successful, so there is no need to change," "We must grow the business to $500 million in 5 years," and "We're customer focused (but only to the extent that it helps us meet our forecasted financial targets)."

In the correct practice of Lean management, the purpose of business is to satisfy customers, even if it might occasionally negatively impact an internal financial or non-financial target. It is not to make money. One of management's jobs is to create shareholder value [4], not maximize shareholder value. There is an attitude that we must change even if we are successful; success should create a greater urgency for improvement in order to blunt complacency. We must grow the business, but growth must be stable and occur over the long-term [5]. It is not sensible to treat customers well when it serves the company's interests and then treat customers poorly when it does not. That's not customer satisfaction.

Business principles that are implied and which are situational do not serve as effective guides for thinking and decision-making. They cause widespread confusion, which then leads to inaction, the signature attribute of conventional management – not of Lean management.

Business principles must be explicit and consistently applied, while those which are at odds with Lean management – be they implicit or explicit – must be modified, de-emphasized, discarded, or replaced.

Business Processes
Lean management has an objective to improve business processes by converting them from push to pull and then achieving flow in pull systems. Operations usually bears the

brunt of efforts to convert from push to pull. But operations does not function in isolation. It must interact, to varying degrees, with all other departments and their business processes. Yet these other departments are typically not challenged to convert their processes from push to pull and to achieve flow. The mash-up, then, is simultaneous operation of the Lean business processes (pull, buyers' market view) and conventional business processes (push, sellers' market view).

Senior managers allow this business process mash-up to linger for years because they are unaware of the details, which is the result of not having participated in kaizen and learning how processes connect to each other. This frustrates people at lower levels who have led efforts to establish pull systems and are trying to get them to flow. It makes it difficult for pull systems to operate smoothly when they encounter batch-and-queue push processes.

This unhappily coexistence is a direct consequence of executives delegating Lean to others, thereby rendering inoperative the feedback loop that comes from hands-on experience.

Metrics
Not recognizing that Lean is a different management system than conventional management has severe implications for business metrics. Executives who embark on a Lean transformation invariably continue to use the metrics they have long used despite their inappropriateness for Lean. Conventional management metrics are rooted in a sellers' market, push production system view of business, which is the opposite of what Lean management is trying to achieve.

Therefore, company- and department-level metrics must be evaluated one-by-one to determine if they are consistent with Lean principles and if they contribute to eliminating waste, unevenness, and unreasonableness. If they do not do that, then the metric must be modified, de-emphasized, discarded, or replaced [6].

Metrics that are famously inconsistent with Lean management are:

- Purchase price variance
- Earned hours
- Machine utilization rate
- Standard costs

These metrics distort reality, disrupt information flows, and cause people to do things that are inconsistent with Lean. They create waste, unevenness and unreasonableness [7], and also generate destructive behavioral waste which contributes to wasteful organizational politics [8]. At the same time, management will ask people to work to a takt time, reduce set-up times, standardize their work, organize into cells to reduce space, reduce inventories, etc. The metric mash-up forces people to make a choice, and the choice they will make will almost always be to satisfy the approved conventional management metric, thus inadvertently undercutting their Lean efforts.

Executives will also misuse financial tools such as return on investment (ROI) and internal rate of return (IRR), which generate metrics used to evaluate the cost-benefit of activities such as kaizen. This shows the claims made by executives that the company is customer-focused are bogus. Further, the use of ROI and IRR provides a widely accepted vehicle for justifying the status quo; to avoid engaging in improvement activities, the result of which is delays and inaction. Executives' claims concerning the importance of continuous improvement are also bogus.

If people see ways to eliminate waste, unevenness and unreasonableness, they should be able to go do it without having to justify their actions to management. Justifications show that management distrusts workers and are a wasteful over-inspection process that can be eliminated.

Training
One of the objectives of Lean management is to make things visible so that people can recognize problems and work to correct them simply and inexpensively. However, the training programs often do not parallel this objective. In fact, they usually run counter to it. Management will approve training courses and programs related to leadership development, for example, which are complicated and expensive, such as emotional intelligence and human resource competency models.

These leadership development programs were created to correct the types of problems found in conventionally managed businesses. So as a business embarks on its Lean transformation, with the requisite Lean training, management may also simultaneously authorize leadership development training that does not directly connect to Lean or is inconsistent with Lean principles and practices. For example, emotional intelligence and human resource competency models, while they can be helpful [9], do not promote kaizen, go see, standardized work, or the elimination of waste, unevenness, and unreasonableness.

So the mash-up here is mixing Lean training with non-Lean training, thus asking people to master both while somehow reconciling gaps and inconsistencies – which will surely occur only on an individual basis. While a few people might be able to reconcile gaps and inconsistencies, most will not be able to. The people who cannot will flounder and likely receive no help from the ones that were successful. Sharing is critical to the success of Lean, but this behavior will likely not be operative because rewards will be as they were under conventional management – largely individual.

Kaizen is a robust training process that teaches people many new things including how to recognize and correct problems, understand process and how they are interconnected, and improve teamwork and leadership skills. Management can avoid the training mash-up by using kaizen as the principal means for training current and future leaders [10], and reduce or eliminate training that is intended for conventionally managed businesses. For this to be effective, kaizen, in its many forms, has to be a daily activity, not a once-in-a-while "event."

In summary, management must avoid the continued use of principles, processes, metrics, and training associated with conventional management. They must also be diligent and avoid importing these into the business. This is especially true when hiring new managers and executives, whose prior experiences will likely be solidly rooted in conventional management principles, practices, and metrics. They can easily cause the organization to backslide by introducing delays and rework, and inhibiting material and information flows.

Notes

[1] Consultants, trainers, and educators are also prone to mash-up management systems and tools.

[2] This does not reflect well on higher education, particularly business schools, whose professors also seem very confused between management systems and management tools. Executives who do not see the problems that mash-ups create, or who advocate mash-ups, have been poorly educated, both formally as undergraduate or graduate students and informally on-the-job or in corporate training. You would expect higher education to teach students the difference between Lean and conventional management systems and how particular tools may or may not be appropriate depending upon the management system in use.

[3] Consultants will surely come to the rescue with an expensive new tool that typically overpromises and under-delivers. See for example, "Enduring Ideas: The Business System," *The McKinsey Quarterly*, June 2009, http://www.mckinseyquarterly.com/Enduring_Ideas_The_business_system_2379

[4] Actually, management's job is to create good products and services. Cash-paying customers are the ones that create shareholder value.

[5] Toyota has stumbled badly in recent years. Its self-imposed high growth period from 1998-2008 seems to be the key factor that has led to numerous problems that will be difficult to correct.

[6] B. Emiliani, with D. Stec, L. Grasso, and J. Stodder, *Better Thinking, Better Results: Case Study and Analysis of an Enterprise-Wide Lean Transformation*, second edition, The CLBM, LLC, Wethersfield, Conn., 2007, pp. 201-229

[7] M.L. Emiliani, D.J. Stec, and L.P. Grasso, "Unintended Responses to a Traditional Purchasing Performance Metric," *Supply Chain Management: An International Journal*, Vol. 10, No. 3, 2005, pp. 150-156.

[8] B. Emiliani, *Practical Lean Leadership: A Strategic Leadership Guide for Executives*, The CLBM, LLC, Wethersfield, Conn., 2008

[9] I received extensive leadership development training in both emotional intelligence and competency models when I worked in industry. While I found them helpful, I also found them lacking with respect to the needs of a Lean business. Over decade later I produced a workbook that is consistent with the needs of current and emerging leaders of Lean businesses called *Practical Lean Leadership*. See note [8].

[10] By this I mean kaizen that is focused on actual doing, not the common corrupted form of kaizen, which is a planning exercise that leads to the

team having to ask for management's permission to eliminate waste, unevenness, and unreasonableness.

Making Deep Problems Visible

Sensei always teaches us that we must make problems visible in order to improve. The great difficulty that most executives have with Lean management tells us that many problems must still be invisible, which deprives executives of the information they need to better understand and correctly practice Lean management. There are at least a dozen deep problems that must be made visible for Lean to thrive.

We have seen so many Lean transformations over the last two or three decades that have failed or have not met expectations that something is obviously wrong. Even without any detailed analysis we can preliminarily conclude that the information executives need to succeed must be very different than the information they have been getting [1]. This suggests Lean transformations are difficult because there are deeper problems which have not been made visible, and that people must not recognize these deep problems as being relevant to Lean management.

Lean management loses its reality-based, "go-see" quality when problems with Lean transformations are not made visible to senior managers. Further, the "Respect for People" principle is not being put into practice when problems remain hidden to those who want to transition to Lean management and become Lean leaders [2]. To have credibility as an alternate capitalist management system with anything more than a niche audience – and to not be perceived as selling a myth – the Lean community must make deep problems visible and provide different information to executives. This has nothing at all to do with Lean tools, so there is no need to spend any more time on that aspect of Lean management.

What are the problems that have not been made visible? Below I have listed 12 items – by no means is it comprehensive – that are organized into three categories: economic, social, and political. These are largely invisible as problems because Lean tools continue to occupy center-stage in most Lean transformations, Lean consulting, and Lean training activities. Importantly, the items listed in these three categories reflect the extent to which adoption of Lean management means changes in management thinking and practice, going far beyond most managers' conception of Lean as simply tools used in operations to achieve 5% year-over-year cost savings [3].

Some of these deep problems will surely be ugly and could also stir-up emotions, but improvement must prevail over personal discomfort. You will learn that what is very useful to the leader of a conventionally managed business is completely useless to Lean leaders. In this dichotomy lay 12 deep problems that I will now make visible.

ECONOMIC

Economic Man
The hyper-simplistic assumption that people are rational self-interested maximizers is a free pass to be consistently selfish and to marginalize or deny the existence of stakeholders – employees, suppliers, customers, investors, communities – all of which are required for the proper functioning of a business [4]. Economic man is wholly inconsistent with the "Continuous Improvement" and "Respect for People" princi-

ples and the Lean view that business must satisfy both human and economic needs. It grossly distorts reality and is therefore useless to Lean leaders who seek a clear view of reality.

Self-interest is also naïvely seen as a helpful, pragmatic way to prevent the occurrence of problems which the self-interested party might be subject to. The logic is that an executive would not make a decision that might harm the company because it would not be in the executive's interest nor the company's interest to do so. However, the global financial crisis of 2007-2009 is only the most recent example of self-interest that has led to personal and corporate ruin. In Lean management, self-interest would immediately be identified as an impractical and ineffective countermeasure, without ever having to actually evaluate it as a countermeasure in practice.

In addition, the belief that unfettered pursuit of self-interest will always promote broader societal interests, is a grave error in logic. The antecedent does not necessarily follow the conclusion; i.e. there could be many other explanations or actions that support the conclusion. Adam Smith recognized that this effect may or may not occur, but his words have been widely misinterpreted [5] to further justify self-interest and transform it from a fault into a virtue in economics.

What this means is that it is time to replace *Atlas Shrugged* as your favorite book [6], in which rational self-interest is presented as a transcendent virtue, with one that teaches how to do 5 Whys root cause analysis. This will help executives understand the very narrow circumstances under which rational self-interest might be acceptable and the broad circumstances under which rational self-interest creates recurring problems that consume large amounts of resources.

Free Markets
Every so often influential economists, politicians, and CEOs come to believe in the absolute authority and inviolable correctness (and efficiency) of markets, a view known as "free market fundamentalism." This is very troublesome to Lean leaders because they dislike fads and groupthink [7], are exceedingly stingy in handing out free passes [8], and thoroughly disdain laissez-faire as a response to problems [9]. Instead, they like to think and take quick, practical actions to correct or avoid problems.

At its core, the market is information. Information can be right, wrong, or inconclusive. Information must be carefully evaluated on a case-by-case basis to determine its quality and validity. The market is not correct just because it is the market, any more that I am correct just because I am a teacher or you are correct just because you are the president of a company. The market is a summary or collective representation of human decisions at points in time, therefore the market is human. We know for certain that humans are fallible, therefore we know for certain that markets are fallible – and that they stumble often and fail periodically.

The human decisions that make up "the market" are based on a combination of people whose decisions are the result of careful detailed study, cursory evaluations, and those who carelessly join the herd. The proportions of these are probably 5% careful detailed study, 30% cursory evaluations, and 65% who join the herd. The herd mentality is likely to prevail often because most people do not have the education, interest, or time to carefully vet information or get deep into the details. So they understandably use shortcuts.

One shortcut is to assume that many people, rather than few, have carefully studied a problem or opportunity, and that market sentiment is based principally on unbiased, high-fidelity, fact-based analysis rather than simple rule-of-thumb or guesses. In other words, the good information is assumed to greatly outweigh bad information. Given the cyclic nature of economic performance, the bad information, made up of shortcuts built on top of shortcuts, must obviously outweigh good information from time to time.

Thinking that the market is always right is a shortcut, a simplistic characterization used to accelerate and confirm decision-making. It is also an excuse and a stark admission of a refusal to ask questions or to study; a refusal to think, which Lean leaders (who are not infallible) try hard not to do.

Individual or collective decision-making is subject to error though decision-making traps [10] such as conforming evidence. This is where information that supports a specific view or desire is accepted while that which contradicts it is immediately discarded. For example: Your objective is to make a lot of money and you are told a certain investment will make you a lot of money. That is what you want to hear, so you then invest your money (think Enron, Bernard Madoff, etc.).

Decision-making traps are the result of shallow thinking or of not thinking at all. This helps explain why the same errors are repeated at the nano-level of personal finance, the micro-level of a business, and the macro-level of national economies. The dogma of free market fundamentalism excuses people from the task, their liberty, of thinking for themselves. Unfortunately, this helps perpetuate a boom-bust economy and prevents us from attaining higher levels of economic quality and long-term performance.

Fortunately, you can be fully capitalist and support free markets without having to support unbridled free markets (see the section on Regulation). Free market fundamentalism and laissez-faire as a response to problems are not pragmatic and are therefore not at all helpful to Lean leaders [11]. Even Adam Smith did not think the "invisible hand" was operating in all circumstances, a concept he did not develop at all and clearly equivocated on because he could not know if its effect was absolute [12].

Regulation
Regulation is nothing more than supervision to assure quality; inspection for conformance to specifications or standards in order to avoid failures. Responsibility for regulation is usually shared between various stakeholders: the company (employees), suppliers, customers, state agency, federal agency, internal auditor (over-inspectors), or external auditor. Many small distributed efforts will yield better results, but not perfect results, compared to one large single effort such as self-regulation by a company.

While people may not like regulation if given a choice, regulation appropriate to the sensible objective of maintaining stability, thus avoiding high peaks and low valleys in performance (such as economic bubbles followed by deep recessions or lapses in quality), helps avoid failures that voraciously consume all forms of resources.

Lean leaders use principles – "Continuous Improvement" and "Respect for People" – as the primary high-level means to regulate activities. They regulate detailed work activities, daily inputs and outputs, using pull systems, standardized work, visual controls, supermarkets, value stream maps, takt time, 5 Whys, A3 reports, policy deployment, etc., to assure product or service integrity.

Things that are important, such as the economy, the long-term viability of our industries, and customer satisfaction need to be prudently regulated [13]. In business, "management controls" are very important and indicates that executives readily accept regulation and most, oddly enough, voluntarily over-regulate (i.e. they go overboard on management controls because they typically do not do formal root cause analysis when problems arise). To suggest that regulations, government or otherwise, do not serve any useful purpose at any level is simply to deny reality. The notion that self-regulation is most effective because it is not in one's interest to do bad things or take shortcuts is illogical reasoning because it is based on false assumptions. Short-term needs and incentives – often badly-designed incentives – can easily trump long-term company or customer interests. All you have to do to confirm this is read *The Wall Street Journal* on any day, or just look inside your own business.

Denying that regulations can be beneficial, minimizing or negating the value of prudent regulation, or thinking that self-regulation is the single most effective solution are seen by Lean leaders as concepts that are detached from reality and offer few or no practical benefits.

Supply-Side Economics
Batch-and-queue production is supply-side economics on a small scale [14] and will lead to overproduction and increased costs. This in turn leads to discounting to stimulate demand of unsold goods (similar to what tax cuts are intended to do in supply-side economics) and reduces profits. Future sales are brought forward which contribute to the bullwhip effect and thus increases sales and production volatility month-to-month. Being supply-driven is less efficient and guarantees higher costs, which forces senior managers to be increasingly zero-sum in their strategies, tactics, and decisions to reduce costs.

Lean leaders seek to become demand-driven to the greatest extent possible, recognizing the reality that they do not live in an ideal world and that it may be impossible to perfectly synchronize supply and demand for most, but not all, goods or services. Lean leaders will strive to become 96-98% or better demand-driven (Keynesian) and 2-4% or less supply-driven, meaning they operate with 7-14 days of inventory.

If a company is successful in becoming demand-driven across the enterprise, then the large amount of cash made available virtually eliminates the need for zero-sum thinking. It also greatly reduces the need to lobby federal and state legislators for tax cuts, which are nothing more than small recurring corporate bailouts to pay for three perpetual assets found in abundance in supply-driven businesses: waste, unevenness, and unreasonableness.

Pay for Performance

Since the time of Frederic Winslow Taylor (late 1800s) [15], pay for performance has proven to be a remarkably difficult thing to do correctly in part because people cheat to obtain better outcomes for themselves or their friends. Pay for performance has proven no less difficult in recent decades for the boards of directors and executives of most of America's largest corporations. These outcomes suggest a need for simplification rather than making performance-based pay plans more complex.

Compensation for senior managers should return to the reality of what is fair and what works. It should be low to moderate, 80% cash-based (10-20 times entry level worker pay) [16], no more than 20% awarded in stock which should vest over 4-5 years, and very limited corporate perks for executives [17]. Compensation for workers should be salary plus quarterly profit sharing, derived from a simple profit sharing formula such as: 15% of pre-tax consolidated income divided by total straight time wages for the quarter [18].

Profit sharing is critical to the success of Lean management. A 3% annual raise pool as a reward for improving productivity 25%, 50%, 100%, or 300% is ridiculous. It will not get workers excited or make them more committed to think, invent, try new things, and ask "why?" Lean management will not work as well as it could without profit sharing, partly because profit sharing supports achieving company-level goals, reinforces teamwork, and is consistent with the "Respect for People" principle.

Most large companies do not have profit sharing, and to institute profit sharing is typically seen by executives as something that is impossible to do because it is money out of shareholders' pockets – a zero-sum view clearly rooted in a deep desire to maintain the status quo. Instead, senior managers must realize that broad-based worker engagement in continuous improvement (with management's participation, CEO on down), in a no-blame environment ("Respect for People" principle), will deliver better economic results for shareholders through improved equity growth and dividend yield. All key stakeholders will prosper. This is what skilled executives do.

SOCIAL

Sharing
Executives often refer to business as a "game," which it is not because people lives – their emotional and physical health – and livelihoods are at stake. Viewing business as a game or as "war" means that managers will draw upon these analogies to define and legitimize their thinking and actions. The principal feature of games and war is that they are intentionally designed to be zero-sum. Business, however, was never designed to be zero-sum [19]. It is made that way by senior managers to simplify their job – to de-skill their job – for which they are highly paid.

Historically, business schools do not teach business as non-zero-sum from a unified pedagogical perspective. I know of no business that uses the Caux Round Table *Principles for Business* [20] as their guiding principles for teaching non-zero-sum business behavior to every employee. While corporate codes of conduct can imply non-zero-sum business behavior, it is rare to actually find it in anything other than isolated examples within a given company. Think about it: Of the 10 or so supervisors you have over the last 10-20 years, have any of them told you that business should be conducted in a non-zero-sum fashion? Probably none. Of the dozen or so supervisors I have had, not one told me that.

Given these facts, it is not surprising that we broadly witness the strategic and tactical conduct of business as zero-sum. Key stakeholders are periodically marginalized by senior managers to satisfy one or more of the company's or management's interests. For example, employees are laid-off or given meager raises, suppliers are squeezed for lower prices, customers receive lower quality goods and services or must pay higher prices, and businesses move offshore to avoid paying taxes. Managers have not been taught and cannot fathom how to run a business in a non-zero-sum fashion. That is the problem with conventional management which Lean management seeks to correct, in part because zero-sum undermines teamwork and causes people to want to work against the company. Why would executives ever do anything to give people reasons to work against the company? Flow cannot be achieved when the key stakeholders are misaligned.

Lean management requires executives to share the wealth among stakeholders, but not necessarily equally. Sharing is not socialism; your parents did not teach you that. Take the case of customers; what do they want? Answer: lower prices and better value. What do employees want? Answer: higher pay, for one thing. What do suppliers want? Answer: fair prices and better communication with their customers. et cetera.

One should not assume that fulfilling these needs comes at

shareholder's expense. If anything, the stakeholders will work together to eliminate the three bad assets of waste, unevenness, and unreasonableness, which will deliver better results to shareholders.

Selfishness is a virtue in conventional management, but not in Lean management.

Fairness
Lean management does not suggest the goal of equality of outcomes among key stakeholders. Rather, the goal is fair outcomes among the key stakeholders: employees suppliers, customers, investors, and communities. Like sharing, fairness is not socialism.

When it comes to employees, are executives prepared to increase real wages 50% over a 20 or 30 year period? Workers want to receive meaningful pay increases for improving productivity, not flat pay or pay cuts [21]. For example, if employees who participate in kaizen improve productivity 25%, 50%, or 100%, they will not expect a 25%, 50%, or 100% increase in wages. But they certainly will not expect a 3% raise pool either; that is perceived by employees as unfair. The reward must be appropriate to the (process and) results to maintain a high interest in participating in kaizen.

Lean leaders are not put-off by the idea of high wages and low cost (i.e. fewer, more productive people that are well-paid versus many less productive people who receive low pay). To them it is not an oxymoron. It makes sense and is not difficult to achieve when people work together to better understand customers' wants and needs, and eliminate the three bad assets of waste, unevenness, and unreasonableness.

Employees also perceive as unfair to be laid-off as a result of participating in kaizen. Rightly so; this is a zero-sum application of kaizen which was never its intent [22]. This conflicts with the "Respect for People" principle and is otherwise just an incredibly stupid thing for executives to do because it chokes off ideas, innovation, and information flow throughout the organization.

Likewise, a reliable and productive supplier should not be told by its biggest customer that it alone must absorb a 30% increase in raw material prices, where raw material accounts for 40% of its costs. To be fair, the customer has to share the burden of cost increases for which suppliers have no control.

Fairness is not a virtue in conventional management, but it is in Lean management. Both fairness and sharing are seen as smart business because they enable flow.

Learning
Conventional management, driven by zero-sum thinking, is deterministic, which is why so many executives practice it. Its simplicity is almost impossible to resist; "I win, you lose," what else is there to know? Certitude is assured, there is never any need to ask "why?", and there is no need to continue learning about business, management, or leadership [23]. This is what allows many senior managers to claim they know business. You will never hear a musician say that about music or a golfer say that about golf. There are really only two challenges to becoming a zero-sum executive: 1) developing the strength to endure the constant criticism that comes

from various stakeholders, and 2) living with yourself. It turns out these are minor challenges because lots of people can do them.

This type of executive is never wrong and never makes any mistakes. "I am right and you are wrong" is zero-sum. Any problems that are experienced are caused by other people who did not understand something or somehow failed in their duties. It's that simple. However, leaders who cannot admit mistakes quickly lack credibility among their followers because it is not human to be mistake-free. Not having credibility among followers is one major mistake that cannot be attributed to anyone other than the leader.

Conversely, the non-zero-sum nature of Lean means it is a non-deterministic management system in which business cannot be distilled to a simple rule-of-thumb. Certitude is not assured. You never hear Lean leaders say they know all there is to know about business, management, or leadership [24]. There is always more to learn, which is consistent with the "Continuous Improvement" and "Respect for People" principles.

Lean leaders make mistakes. Mistakes are good because they are the basis for learning and improvement. Lean leaders want mistakes to be made visible so that they can be corrected. They take responsibility when other people did not understand something or when others failed in their duties. There are more than two challenges to becoming a non-zero-sum Lean leader, but let's start with these: 1) developing the strength to ask why and endure constant self-reflection, and 2) living with the high expectations that you set for yourself for learning and improving every day.

Practicing the "Continuous Improvement" and "Respect for People" principles are high-level challenges which few are willing to do because it means having to learn too many new things. It means to become skilled.

Leadership

Ask yourself the question: "Who were the best bosses I ever had?" If you have worked in industry for 15 or 20 years, you have probably had at least 10 bosses. Maybe two out of the 10 were these best you ever had, and I am sure you remember them warmly. Ask yourself another question: "What were the qualities and characteristics of these two bosses?" Invariably you will say they were trusting, humble, calm, listened well, gave useful feedback often, patient, objective, consistent, wise, supportive, and had good humor. Think of the other eight bosses; what qualities and characteristics did they have? Typically they will have characteristics such as authoritarian, blaming, judgmental, yells at people, intimidating, disrespectful, manipulative, bullying, condescending, self-centered, etc.

Now ask yourself: "Who would I rather report to, the best boss or the worst boss?" Naturally, it would be the best boss. Why? It is because the best boss behaves in ways that subordinates prefer. But there is more to it than just that. The best bosses behave in a non-zero-sum fashion, and by doing so they enable information flow and teamwork, which makes people to want to get involved in continuous improvement and other activities. These managers make work fun and satisfying.

The bad bosses, on the other hand, cause people to withhold information, focus selfishly on themselves, and discourage participation in continuous improvement and other activities because people will get blamed if something goes wrong [25] or lose their job if they are successful. The characteristics of bad bosses are almost uniformly zero-sum which discourages learning the kinds of things that will help the company and its key stakeholders prosper long-term. They make work difficult and very unsatisfying.

Workers do not ask bad bosses to behave the way they do; there is no pull for bad boss behaviors. Instead, the bad bosses push their bad behaviors onto their subordinates and others. If there is no pull for wasteful leadership behaviors, then why do it? The leaders of conventionally managed business generally behave in wasteful, zero-sum ways that add cost but do not add value. Recognize also that it is bad for one's physical and mental health to behave in zero-sum ways, and bad for the health of workers as well. Bad bosses clearly do not respect themselves or other people. As companies try to control healthcare costs, they surely should begin at home by behaving in non-zero sum ways, starting with the top executives.

In contrast, Lean leaders embrace the "Respect for People" principle and realize that they must behave differently, in non-zero-sum ways, to be consistent with their ongoing calls to eliminate waste, unevenness, and unreasonableness. So they try to behave in the least wasteful way they can at any given point in time, reflect upon their strengths and weaknesses, and strive to continuously improve their leadership behaviors, skills, and capabilities. This type of non-zero-sum leadership makes people want to work together, promotes learning, and develops people. So, to be an effective Lean leader means one's focus must shift from relying on wasteful behaviors to get things done to using value-added behaviors.

Please don't make the false assumption that value-added leadership behaviors will be too expensive or that it will take longer to get things done. Whatever downside you can imagine is probably inaccurate.

POLITICAL

Corporate Purpose

The purpose of the corporation must be carefully thought through because it can lead to widespread organizational dysfunction and generate internal discord between factions that seek to satisfy shareholders and those that seek to satisfy external (cash-paying) customers. To most executives the purpose of the corporation is singular: to make money or to maximize shareholder value. Note that these are assumed to be true, based on faith or authority, without any proof of their validity [26]. No doubt making money is very important, but to have that as the corporations' sole purpose fails to energize employees other than a top few executives. The result will be patchy teamwork, poor information flow, and many other problems that will accumulate over time and eventually lead to distress – usually coincident with an economic downturn. So the corporate purpose, "to make money" is not a good one to embrace.

What about "maximizing shareholder value"? It's a nice cliché, not the result of rigorous analysis, and is not actually doable in the real world – nor is it advisable to even try. Firstly, maximizing one thing, shareholder value, means minimizing other things, namely the interests of other stakeholders. The cliché drives management to be zero-sum in its strategies and tactics, typically short-term. Secondly, we must look at the details of the shareholder value equation to understand what it actually means to maximize shareholder value [27]:

$$\text{Shareholder Value} = \text{Corporate Value} - \text{Debt}$$

"Shareholder value" obviously represents investors, which can be owners, executives, employees, joint-venture partners, suppliers, etc.; "Corporate value" is determined by customers who pay cash for products or services, typically end-use customers; and "Debt" represents outstanding obligations that the corporation has to its employees (paychecks, benefits, etc.), suppliers (invoices), and community (taxes). To maximize shareholder value, debt must be minimized, in the limit by taking "Debt" to zero which is not achievable in the real world.

While on the one hand being financially over-leveraged, executives make great efforts to reduce current and future debts by laying off employees (often elective), squeezing suppliers on prices; moving offshore to avoid taxes, etc. This is not a formula for long-term business success, and it is of course inconsistent with the "Respect for People" principle. Enron executives, for example, believed that their corporate purpose was singular: to maximize shareholder value. The dysfunction that ensued among executives contributed greatly to Enron's downfall.

This logical analysis tells us that companies do not exist for purely financial reasons, to make money or to maximize shareholder value. Business was created by people to serve human interests, and business does not happen without people. Therefore, better reasoning tells us that corporate purpose cannot be singular, but must be dual [28]: corporations exists for human and economic reasons, which is consistent with why the state grants people charters to organize businesses; to do good work for humans (society) in ways that will be profitable. That is the perspective of Lean leaders.

Given that corporate value is largely defined by the cash flow resulting from cash-paying customers, it is much more sensible to put customers at the center of a corporation's purpose, not investors. Specifically, a purpose which seeks to satisfy customers' wants and needs. A corporate purpose to "satisfy customers" would be preferable. This means that executives should focus on serving customers, and everyone in the enterprise should work to find ways to better serve customers [29]. It is no surprise that companies that serve customers well have higher growth rates and are more profitable, which serves the interests of investors and the other key stakeholders. This is consistent with the "Respect for People" principle.

Organizational Politics

Most people dislike organizational politics because they see it as time-consuming and as a distraction from getting real work done. Despite this, executives accept organizational politics as if it is a naturally occurring phenomenon that cannot be reduced or eliminated. People who are troubled by organizational politics are told by their boss to "get used to it" or "you need to grow a thicker skin." Executives who condone, and more likely foment, organizational politics truly don't understand the damage that this zero-sum behavior does, nor do they believe in improvement or respecting people. Their satisfaction with the status-quo is stunning given their constant calls for change.

Organizational politics is much more than a waste of time or a distraction, it immobilizes people and information. It prevents people from doing important things such as recognizing problems, developing problem-solving skills, and learning the types of things needed to contribute to the long-term success of the company. It causes corporate blindness and paralysis, and thus prevents management from seeing the reality of whatever situation confronts them and acting upon it in a timely manner. Executives in organizations that are highly political spend a tremendous amount of time creating and maintaining false appearances. This is time taken from seeing how things really are; it drives highly paid executives to "go play" instead of "go see." Playing games is not what they are being paid to do.

Lean leaders see organizational politics for what it is: a wasteful leadership behavior, one that adds cost but does not add value. Try answering the question: "How does organizational politics benefit the customers who pay for and use our products and services?" The answer is simple: it does not benefit customers in any way. In fact, it harms customers because organizational politics blocks the flow of information, slows decision-making, increases costs, and makes the company less aware of their customers' changing wants and needs. This can be deadly in that it will surely lead to severe financial distress at some point (think Xerox circa 1999) and perhaps bankruptcy (think General Motors in 2009).

Similarly, organizational politics does not benefit employees, suppliers, or investors. Organizational politics leads to many costly errors, most of which are repeat errors, which management typically corrects in a zero-sum manner by making employees, suppliers, customers, or investors pay for the errors. Employees will get laid off, suppliers will get squeezed, cash flow declines, share price drops, and dividends get cut; outcomes that could have been avoided by "go see" leadership.

Organizational politics is not a naturally occurring phenomenon. It is purposefully created by humans, perhaps driven by extroverts to create even more thrilling workplaces, and therefore can be eliminated. Top executives eliminate organizational politics by recognizing that it is waste, by establishing a no-blame policy (and making it come alive every day), and by practicing the "Continuous Improvement" and "Respect for People" principles. Organizational politics will not go away overnight, but senior managers can make steady progress towards reducing and virtually eliminating it in less than one year.

Lifting the fog of organizational politics will reveal a new world, perhaps in some ways a bit uglier than you would like, but it enables you to see the challenges clearly so you can respond to them in a timely manner. Executives are constantly saying that resources are limited and that costs must be reduced, so why allow organizational politics to consume time, money [30], and other valuable resources such as employees lives?

Politicizing and Bureaucratizing Lean
One common feature of Lean transformation is the efforts made by most senior managers to politicize and bureaucratize

Lean. They do this by establishing levels of Lean achievement, certification of Lean facilitators, and account for Lean
activities using wrong methods and metrics. Given the broad
acceptance for organizational politics and bureaucracies, it is
not surprising that most managers would politicize and
bureaucratize Lean just as they would do to anything else.

This is not helpful towards getting people to participate in the
daily application of Lean principles and practices. In most
cases, it quickly degenerates in to a game between management and the workers and develops into a false representation
of organizational capabilities; the improvement charts look
very nice but the company cannot perform because the people have not actually learned Lean management – they are
gaming the system to survive the situation that their leaders
have unfortunately placed them into.

Requiring the achievement of discrete levels of Lean-ness in a
work area instantaneously reveals management's complete
lack of understanding of what continuous improvement means.
Reaching the top level suggests to workers they can stop or at
least slow down efforts to improve, and invites management to
gloat. The guaranteed outcome is backslide. Certifications,
unfortunately, do not mean that people will actually do what
they have been certified to do. While that may be management's expectation, the lack of rewards or presence of disin-
centives, even very subtle ones, will discourage those who
have been certified. In addition, certifications create distinc-
tions between people that can undercut teamwork.

Basing the decision to have a week-long kaizen on the
requirement to achieve some arbitrary return on investment or

internal rate of return target is a misuse of financial tools and shows that management utterly, completely, and categorically misunderstands of the meaning and intent of kaizen. Customers do not care about a company's internal targets. They care about whether or not the product or service has features they want, is available when they want it, has the quality they expect, and gives them value for their money. Kaizens that achieve the requisite return on investment for the company may not deliver to customers any of the things that they want. Kaizens should take place because of the never-ending need to improve value for customers and eliminate waste, unevenness, and unreasonableness – not on achieving an arbitrary return on investment target.

Further, kaizen is the process by which people learn to recognize and correct problems. Turning kaizen into yet another financial tool narrowly focused on achieving short-term cost reduction means people will go through the motions but they will not learn. Kaizen is much more than just process improvement to obtain cost reduction. It improves information flow; it creates a culture that asks "why?; it overcomes decision-making traps; it promotes innovation; it improves people's understanding of the work; it reduces barriers to interacting across functions; it helps identify future leaders; and it makes senior managers smarter – but only if they, too, participate in kaizen.

Executives who politicize and bureaucratize Lean management are actually practicing conventional management and misusing some Lean tools and processes. They are also defeating people's will to improve. Senior managers have a lot of work to do if they wish to become skilled Lean leaders [31].

. . . . .

What I have done in the preceding pages is highlight some of the ways conventional managers think and how they do things, and contrasted these to how Lean leaders think and do things. I have earnestly, but surely not perfectly, explained how each item is a problem that needs to be made visible in order to achieve more successful Lean transformations. In a nutshell, Lean leaders have no use for impractical economic, social, or political concepts [32].

The dozen items I have presented are similar to a golf handicap. If you subscribe to the conventional management view for each of the 12 items, then you are a 12-handicap businessperson (and don't forget there are many more than just these 12 items). The larger the handicap, the less capable the golfer – or leader. Executives should want to strive to bring their handicap to zero to become at least a "scratch" (Lean) businessperson.

The good news is that you can methodically reduce your business handicap a lot easier than you can reduce your golf handicap. You do this by studying Lean management (only the good books, please), by daily application of Lean principles and practices, and by frequently participating in kaizen. The old adage that the devil is in the details could not be more wrong. It is the opportunities and benefits that are in the details. Executives must pay attention to the many small details, as this chapter has tried to show.

Most senior managers will say: "It's too hard," "I don't have time," "We don't need to change," etc. Apparently they prefer the heroics of cleaning up a mess after it has been created rather than doing the unheralded work of avoiding the mess from the start.

If reality is not your bag, then that may be OK for you personally, but as a leader it is not OK for the company, its employees, suppliers, customers, investors, or the communities in which the business operates. Executives who are in it for the money, short-term, will never be motivated by these or any other arguments. Those who care about doing a better job might be moved to improve how they think and work.

Executives know it is a challenging business environment and often speak of the need for speed, flexibility, adaptability to change, etc. These are good capabilities to have in a cyclic economy, but conventional management will not help you achieve them. Executives who are not willing to learn new things and improve will instead periodically hire top-tier consultants and overpay them to install the latest flavor of the month. Their work will always leave the company more vulnerable to a cyclic economy because they address only the symptoms of problems. They do not make deep problems visible.

Notes

[1] This includes erroneous characterizations of Lean as: just a bunch of tools for manager's tool kit, something you do only in operations, kaizen events or projects, as a method to reduce costs, a way to reduce inventories, etc. For a spectacular example of the type of incorrect and misleading information proffered by a top-tier consultancy and therefore consumed by senior managers, see "From Lean to Lasting: Making Operational Improvements Stick," D. Fine, M. Hansen, and S. Roggenhofer, *The McKinsey Quarterly*, McKinsey & Company, November 2008

[2] This effects not only executives but employees and other stakeholders as well.

[3] Operations should never be the only part of the organization that is challenged to improve processes and produce recurring cost savings. Executives should require human resources, finance, MIS, legal, engineering, etc., to do the same. Executives themselves should also do the same in each of the processes that they participate in.

[4] When business is good, executives of large companies generally disdain stakeholders other than investors, but when business is bad executives will immediately embrace all key stakeholders in an effort to gain their support to help the company survive tough times. This duplicitous treatment results from the view that stakeholders are instruments to be manipulated rather than essential components for the successful functioning of business in good times and bad. Viewing key stakeholders as instruments is not conducive to building long-term, mutually beneficial relationships.

[5] A. Smith, *The Wealth of Nations*, 1776, Bantam Classic Edition, March 2003, Bantam Dell, New York, NY, p. 572. "By pursuing his own interest he frequently [but not exclusively] promotes that of the society more effectually than when he really intends to promote it." Smith is not presenting the connection between self-interest and positive impact on society as an axiom, a self-evident truth that requires no proof, as is frequently misinterpreted.

[6] *Atlas Shrugged*, written by Ayn Rand (1957), an emigrant to the United States from communist Russia, is a favorite among many executives and economists. Self-interest in no way guarantees only favorable outcomes; it can just as easily lead to unfavorable outcomes.

[7] H. Okuda, "Slashing Payrolls Shows Executive Incompetence," *JapanEcho*, December 1999, pp. 14-17 and N. Kunio, "Respecting Human Beings: An Interview with Okuda Hiroshi," *LookJapan*, January 2000

[8] "The Toyota Way 2001," Toyota Motor Corporation, internal document,

Toyota City, Japan, April 2001

[9] In the words of Fujio Cho, the past president and current chairman of Toyota Motor Corporation: "The worst evil is not changing – there is nothing worse than doing nothing." Source: http://www.autofieldguide.com/articles/120303.html

[10] J. Hammond, R. Keeney, and H. Raiffa, "The Hidden Traps in Decision-Making," *Harvard Business Review*, September-October 1998, Volume 76, Issue 5, pp. 47-54

[11] Kiichiro Toyoda, the founder of Toyota Motor Corporation, was a strong supporter of free markets. See B. Emiliani, *REAL LEAN: The Keys to Sustaining Lean Management*, Volume Three, The CLBM, LLC, Wethersfield, Conn., 2008, pp. 75-77

[12] A. Smith, *The Wealth of Nations*, 1776, Bantam Classic Edition, March 2003, Bantam Dell, New York, NY, p. 572. "By preferring the support of domestic to that of foreign industry, he intends only his own security; and by directing that industry in such a manner as its produce may be of the greatest value, he intends only his own gain, and he is in this, as in many other cases [but not all cases], led by an invisible hand to promote an end which was no part of his intention." Smith is not presenting the "invisible hand" as an axiom, a self-evident truth that require no proof. For all its support among economists, the words "invisible hand" appear only *once* in *The Wealth of Nations* – a book that is over 1000 pages long. The importance of these two words is immensely overstated by economists who seek to equate selfishness with the common good, in order to justify aggrandizement of wealth (and power) among the few and marginalize the many. It would be as if I wrote a 1000 page book containing the words "big fart" in only one place and then a clique used my two words (i.e. "He is led by a big fart to promote an end which was no part of his intention.") to forever justify their ideological position and achieve their narrow desired outcomes.

[13] Many economists have a bizarre and impractical view that when a major macroeconomic problem occurs, the failure is, by definition, in the past and any future failure will not happen in exactly the same way. Therefore, new regulations that might be applied to correct the problem and avoid future failures are immediately obsolete and will only place new costly burdens on business. That is the same as saying the airplane crashed, and the next accident will not happen in exactly the same way. Therefore, new regulations that might be applied to correct the problem and avoid future airplane crashes are immediately obsolete and will only place new costly burdens on business. The flying public would be outraged at this ineffective approach to public safety. They expect a fair and detailed investigation

and the application of appropriate corrective actions and regulations, if needed, to prevent future failures. The public should demand the same of macroeconomic failures, but economists under the spell of flawed theories put up enormous resistance. Economists are essentially saying, "the problem is too difficult, and there is no assurance that any solution will be helpful, so don't do anything at all," thereby extending laissez faire thinking to problem solving – just do nothing! The acceptance of the flawed logic of do nothing among many economists is stunning and indicates they are more social (i.e. clique-driven) than scientist. Separately, with respect to individual companies, note that managers themselves are part of the regulatory apparatus of a corporation and that they own all policies and metrics (many of them bad) whose intent and effect is to regulate business activities. If top managers really disdain regulation, then they would have a minimum of overhead executive, management, and supervisory positions. But this usually is not the case. The management ranks have swelled in recent years compared to the number workers who actually add value to the products or services that customers buy.

[14] The standard cost accounting system is itself an incentive to produce even if demand is slack. Financial incentives such as reducing various taxes can add to management's incentive to overproduce (and, by the logic of standard cost accounting, this will lower costs which will in turn results in lower prices that will then stimulate demand).

[15] F.W. Taylor, *Shop Management*, Harper & Brothers Publishers, New York, NY, 1911, pp. 21-29. Originally published as "Shop Management" in *Transactions of The American Society of Mechanical Engineers*, Volume XXIV, No. 1003, 1903, pp. 1337-1456

[16] Top executives are not superstars, as the 2008-2009 financial crisis has yet again taught us. The caliber of their work is ordinary at best and in no way worth 100-500 times the average worker's pay as it has been for the last 10-15 years in America's 500 largest corporations. Also, the 10-20 times entry level worker pay figure makes executives accountable for their long-term efforts to depress real wages for workers (see note [21]). If 10-20 times entry level worker pay is not enough for senior managers, then they should increase real wages for workers. Finally, 10-20 times entry level worker pay would result in a huge cost savings for executive labor.

[17] Even at 10-20 times entry level worker pay, executives make a lot of money and can pay for their own, car, auto insurance, life insurance, club memberships, etc.

[18] See *Better Thinking, Better Results: Case Study and Analysis of an Enterprise-Wide Lean Transformation*, B. Emiliani, with D. Stec, L.

Grasso, and J. Stodder, second edition, The CLBM, LLC, Wethersfield, Conn., 2007, pp. 124-126

[19] Business likely began as fair trade between hunter-gatherers. It is not hard to imagine that early-on in the practice of fair trade a wise-ass hunter-gatherer thought he could score a better deal for himself by taking advantage of his trading partner.

[20] The Caux Round Table *Principles for Business* can be found at http://www.cauxroundtable.org

[21] Real wages for workers increased 40% between 1946 and 1974, and -5% from 1976-2007 (source: BLS). These numbers tell you there has been an enormous shift in wealth from workers to those in the upper income categories. Substantially increasing wages for workers should not be a problem if senior management is truly committed to growing the business.

[22] The literal translation of kaizen is "change for the better," in a multilateral context. That means kaizen must not result in negative outcomes for internal or external stakeholders.

[23] As a result of this view, executives often fail keep up with the literature of their chosen profession: management and leadership. This is amazing. It would be as if your physician said "I know everything about internal medicine" and therefore sees no need to keep up-to-date with emerging treatments and new research findings in *The Journal of the American Medical Association*. You would view your doctor as incompetent and search for a new physician. Yet top executives can essentially declare themselves ignorant (at minimum) and perhaps even incompetent, and still be respected and have a high-paying job.

[24] Lean managers are more humble and can easily admit they do not know all there is to know about business. This compels them to be more actively engaged in learning on-the-job, in classroom settings, and by reading books and journal articles on management and leadership (and being careful to ignore that which conflicts with the "Continuous Improvement" and "Respect for People" principles). In addition, Lean leaders also see it as their duty to act as teachers to develop future generations of Lean leaders. In contrast, executives schooled in conventional management do not typically view teaching as part of their day-to-day responsibilities.

[25] Blame is an emotional response, not a fact-based response. Blame reveals that the leader thinks people are the problem, and shows that the leader is not actually thinking and not doing any root cause analysis. You cannot be an effective leader of people if you think people are the problem.

[26] The argument that companies exist to maximize shareholder value can

easily be disproved using simple mathematical logic. See M.L. Emiliani, "A Mathematical Logic Approach to the Shareholder vs. Stakeholder Debate," *Management Decision*, Vol. 39, No. 8, 2001, pp. 618-622. Further, the "finance Mulligan" that executives take every quarter on operating earnings obscures whether any shareholder value has actually been created: EBITDARCMFWCSX... earnings before interest, taxes, depreciation, amortization, restructuring, capex, mistakes, failures, the weather, our customers, our suppliers, and other any other problem that we can assign a cost to that investment analysts will go along with.

[27] A. Rappaport, *Creating Shareholder Value*, The Free Press, New York, NY, 1998

[28] That corporations exists for human and economic reasons fits with the notion of "balance" which pervades Lean thinking. Balance is necessary to avoid extreme conditions. Some examples of balance in Lean management include: the "Continuous Improvement" principle balanced by the "Respect for People" principle; level loading; percent loading chart; job rotation; skills matrix; standard work in process; takt time; etc.

[29] Executives must also be very careful in establishing goals. Establishing a company-centered goal of being #1, just for the sake of being #1, is no good because customers do not care about that. They are more interested in competence and having their wants and needs satisfied as their desires change over time. Another unwise goal is to set a target date or target level of achievement for when the company will be Lean. Becoming Lean is not an end unto itself and gives the impression that Lean is deterministic; that you can one day know Lean. This way of thinking is at odds with the "Continuous Improvement" and "Respect for People" principles.

[30] People often say "time is money." Technically, time is not money because money is bidirectional, it can increase or decrease in value, while time goes in only one direction. It would be more accurate to say: "Time can be monetized."

[31] See for example: B. Emiliani, *Practical Lean Leadership: A Strategic Leadership Guide for Executives*, The CLBM, LLC, Wethersfield, Conn., 2008; *Better Thinking, Better Results: Case Study and Analysis of an Enterprise-Wide Lean Transformation*, B. Emiliani, with D. Stec, L. Grasso, and J. Stodder, second edition, The CLBM, LLC, Wethersfield, Conn., 2007; and B. Emiliani, *REAL LEAN: Learning the Craft of Lean Management*, Volume Four, The CLBM, LLC, Wethersfield, Conn., 2008. See also T. Ohno, *Toyota Production System*, Productivity Press, Portland, OR, 1988; Y. Monden, *Toyota Management System: Linking the Seven Key*

Functional Areas, Productivity Press, Portland, OR, 1993; M. Cowley and E. Domb, *Beyond Strategic Planning: Effective Corporate Action with Hoshin Planning*, Butterworth-Heinemann, New York, NY, 1997; S. Basu, *Corporate Purpose: Why it Matters More than Strategy*, Garland Publishing, New York, NY, 1999; T. Fujimoto, *The Evolution of a Manufacturing System at Toyota*, Oxford University Press, New York, NY, 1999; B. Maskell and B. Baggaley, *Practical Lean Accounting*, Productivity Press, New York, NY, 2003; J. Liker, *The Toyota Way*, McGraw-Hill, New York, NY, 2004; S. Hino, *Inside the Mind of Toyota*, Productivity Press, New York, NY, 2006; J. Liker and M. Hoseus, *Toyota Culture*, McGraw-Hill, New York, NY, 2008; and F.G. Woollard with B. Emiliani, *Principles of Mass and Flow Production*, 55th Anniversary Special Reprint Edition, The CLBM, LLC, Wethersfield, Conn., 2009.

[32] Adherents to the doctrine of "originalism" in law would, if this same doctrine were applied to business, recognize that Lean management (when correctly understood and applied) is a better representation of business as it was originally conceived in both intent and meaning: i.e. non-zero-sum. The "Living business" doctrine, on the other hand, would view the intent and meaning of business as changeable over time, depending on the perspective of individual chief executives: i.e. business as a human-economic activity or business as a purely economic activity whose purpose is to maximize shareholder value (principally short-term). The "living business" doctrine has prevailed since the early 1980s, and periodically before that, and has contributed greatly to ongoing corporate complexity, disorder, and distress, and has also led to national or global financial crises.

4 Work Together

One of the unfavorable consequences of task specialization and cost accounting is the compartmentalization of work activities such that people in a given department will tend to work more among themselves than they will work together with people in other departments. Annual employee appraisals focusing on individual performance and individual rewards contribute to an erosion of skills needed for working together productively with other people. That, coupled with shifting objectives, unclear expectations, uncertain rewards, and fear of being blamed for problems causes people to avoid working together – despite management's constant calls for teamwork.

Lean management is usually practiced incorrectly in ways that more closely resemble conventional management (i.e. Fake Lean), and thus make it difficult for people to want to work together. People will prefer to work in isolation whenever they can, which delays the recognition and correction of problems. No business can afford the time and resources consumed by undetected and recurring problems.

Lean management practiced correctly helps eliminate these problems and promotes higher levels of teamwork than can be achieved in a conventionally managed business or in a Fake Lean business. This leads to much more effective responses to systemic and day-to-day problems, and gives workers a greater appreciation of one another's knowledge, skills, and capabilities. More work of higher quality gets done much faster.

Management must ensure that it understands and practices Lean correctly – especially kaizen – so that people inside and outside the company will want to work together.

Free Money, Free Love

*Every Lean advocate is very enthusiastic about their work.
But individual enthusiasm without extensive, high-level
coordinated group activities to promote Lean management
in policy circles will relegate Lean to a niche practice.
We can do better than that.*

What's in a name?

In October 2007, the Lean Enterprise Institute held a celebration in Cambridge, Massachusetts, to commemorate its 10th anniversary. Jim Womack spoke at the beginning of the event and offered a wonderful retrospective of LEI's beginnings, accomplishments, and future direction, which was to move beyond Lean tools and start to focus on Lean management (finally!). He also shared his regrets over the name "Lean," saying that it was not a good name in hindsight but it is the name we have and should make the best of it. To me, he sounded nearly apologetic.

While Jim's honesty was admirable, he should not have expressed any regret over the name "Lean." Why? The long-view of history tells us that no matter what you call progressive management, executives will resist it or misinterpret and misapply it. John Krafcik could have instead named Lean "Free Money, Free Love" and people would still find reasons to ignore or disparage it. This is not a simple name or branding problem; the challenge runs much deeper than that, as I shall soon explain.

For over 100 years, different names have been given to new

ems and methods. These include: Scientific
  Quality Management, Reengineering, etc.
    ...ent is to introduce progressive management
practices to businesses and organizations. They seek to move
executives away from wasteful conventional management
principles and practices to new ones, which, if understood
and practiced correctly, would do less harm and lead to
greater prosperity for all key stakeholders.

But, as history has shown us time and time again, most managers resist efforts to adopt new business principles and
reform long-established practices, or they misunderstand and
incorrectly practice them. The Hollywood film titled "The
Matrix" offers an interesting analogy [1]. The human charac-
ter Neo (Thomas Anderson, played by Keanu Reeves) and his
colleagues embark on a mission to improve the human condition. They represent a threat to the software in the machine-
based system, which responds by unleashing agents (comput-
er programs) and sentinels (machines) to disrupt or destroy
Neo's mission.

Progressive management, or Neo-management (new management) [2], and the people that introduce it, are often similarly
perceived as threats. To address these threats, some executives (agents) and mid-level managers (sentinels) will disrupt
or destroy their mission to improve the human condition in
business. As in the movie, agents and sentinels appear in
overwhelming numbers to preserve their system. The people
who respond to the threat of Neo-management are not bad
people. They are simply defending what they know to be true;
that which in their minds is settled.

In law there is a principle called "stare decisis," which means to stand by a decision or precedent. It is referred to informally as "settled law." Stare decisis obligates the legal community to accept the decision of a higher court in legal proceedings in lower courts deciding similar cases. Settled law is a practical principle, for without it no legal decision would ever be final and every decision would always be up for review. Precedent would have no meaning or value and the legal system would be unproductive. Settled law imparts predictability to the legal system and provides a stable basis for thought, analysis, and progress.

The same concept applies in business: I call it "settled business." There are economic, social, and political precedents that for practical purposes – meaning for day-to-day business in the real world – are settled. Importantly, advocates of any system of progressive management have consistently failed to appreciate the extent to which, in the minds of most executives, business is settled.

Settled business with respect to economic precedents includes: economic order quantities, economies of scale, standard cost accounting, supply-driven production (similar to supply-side economics), low wages means low costs, unit price savings results in lower costs, economic man, efficient markets, free and unfettered markets, deregulation, etc.

Settled business with respect to social precedents includes: zero-sum thinking (e.g. little or no sharing), people are the problem, blame people for errors, organizational politics, little need for fairness, there is a shortage of management talent, etc.

Settled business with respect to political precedents includes:
short-term thinking, what gets measured gets managed, business is complex, the imperative for growth, pay for performance, environmental responsibility adds cost, and the purpose of business is to make money or to maximize shareholder value.

These precedents can fit within more than one category at a time.

Acceptance for each one of these precedents is very high
among influential people such as senior managers, academics, business journalists, political leaders, economists, and
investors, to name a few. They know these to be true, they
will strenuously defend them, and they will marginalize or
remove those who dissent. They see these as binding precedents; binding principally as a result of their training in
school and on-the-job work experience; binding as a result of
pre-existing company policies, procedures, and metrics; binding as a result of enterprise software systems and machinery;
and binding as a result of people's expectations (such as
investor's expectations). There are no issues here that need to
be re-visited or corrected. Further, what would be gained personally or professionally, late in one's career, by revisiting
these precedents?

Every person who has advocated some form of progressive
management has asked the management in power to question
different aspects of settled business; to overturn established
business precedence. They are asking executives to willingly
re-examine dozens of ideas, principles, practices, tools, methods, and metrics. The vast majority view doing this as costly
and time consuming, and simply unnecessary. Executives are

unwilling to revisit that which they think they have gotten right and which they see working well-enough every day.

What advocates of progressive management have long recognized is that unlike the law, these precedents are non-binding – even though executives and other stakeholders may see them as binding (in part due the inaccurate perception of high switching costs). Since most, if not all of the precedents related to conventional management are non-binding, they can indeed be changed.

However, the past and current approaches that advocates of progressive management have taken to ask executives to overturn established business precedence have obviously been inadequate. The barriers to correcting precedent are much more formidable than the weak, scattershot strategies and tactics employed by the Lean community thus far, and which are easily blunted by anti-Lean actors using elementary forms of illogical thinking such as: red herrings, abusing tradition or expertise, avoiding the force of reason, making false assumptions, creating false dilemmas, expediency, proof before consideration, and ad hominem attacks – often in combination with one another.

We must recognize that what we have been doing is pretty much the same as what advocates of progressive management did in the 10 decades before Lean as we know it today came along (circa 1975). In essence, we have committed to climbing the highest mountain, but are doing so dressed in Hawaiian shirts, shorts, flip-flops, and with some zinc oxide on our noses. Our desire for broad-based adoption of Lean management greatly outstrips our level of preparedness. How then can we realistically expect to be successful?

We must prepare anew for the incredible mountain ahead of us. I propose a fundamental re-thinking of the Lean community's "go to market" strategies and tactics – especially in light of Toyota's recent stumble [3], which only strengthens the positions of the legions of managers who support "settled business."

It seems, at a minimum, that we must work together much more closely, better utilize available resources, and strive to have an impact on policy at the national level. This means that we must spend more time together planning so that execution is more focused and, ultimately, more successful, and so that our Lean stories inspire others and instill confidence.

It also means that we need to get influential economists, from the left, middle, and right, to deeply understand flow [4] because that is who top executives listen to.

Notes

[1] The first two Matrix movies appropriately featured songs from the band Rage Against the Machine, whose purpose is to raise awareness of social, economic, and political injustice. In the context of this article, the injustice is zero-sum conventional management practices. Progressive, non-zero-sum Lean management represents a more just management system.

[2] Many people have heard of the famous Japanese consulting firm Shingijutsu Co., Ltd. Their name, "Shingijutsu," means "new technology," in reference to the new *management* technology that Toyota's production system represents.

[3] Toyota Motor Corporation suffered a severe mismatch between supply and demand in all of its largest markets starting in mid-2008 through mid-2009. This indicates that instead of building to dealer and end-use customer demand, Toyota was instead producing according to a plan. This is just one of many inconsistencies with both the "Continuous Improvement" and "Respect for People" principles in the "Toyota Way 2001" document ("The Toyota Way 2001," Toyota Motor Corporation, internal document, Toyota City, Japan, April 2001).

[4] See "Toyota's British Influence" in Section 1.

Pulling Out Saplings

Lean management offers a proven way for companies to get out of debt – and not just financial debt. Equally important are the non-financial debts of time, quantity, and information. It takes well trained people working over the long-term to reduce and maintain low levels of non-financial debt. Dismissing trained people to meet short-term cost savings targets will leave a company forever in deep debt.

When we think of being in debt, we think of financial debt. We have learned a hard lesson in the Great Recession of 2007-2009 that debt is not as good as the financial engineers made it out to be. Banks that had a conservative 10:1 leverage (10 dollars in debt for every dollar of asset) in the 1980s and 1990s piled on debt and became over-leveraged, as much as 30:1 or more. Their risk increased tremendously, taking the company from a robust financial condition to a weakened condition with no margin for error when the economy falters. Many manufacturing and services businesses fell into this trap and also became over-leveraged.

Given that the macroeconomic situation is unstable and could remain so for some time into the future, it would be wise to de-leverage. From my mechanical engineering education, I learned that exact mathematical calculations should be tempered by safety factors to account for unknowns and to avoid human injury. The concept of safety factor does not exist in business – especially in corporate finance. Therefore, financial reserves are usually inadequate, and 30:1 leverage is simply idiotic. From my perspective, 10:1 leverage is still too much debt for a company to bear, especially in light of continuing economic volatility.

There are others forms of debt – non-financial debt – that executives are much less aware of: time, quantity, and information. Specifically, lead-time, inventories, and the information that people need to get work done. We know from analyzing processes that the value-added time in producing a product or service is short, usually minutes in duration, compared to lead-time that is days or weeks in duration. If the value-added time is 15 minutes and the lead time is 20 days (18,000 minutes assuming a 2-shift operation), then that is a leverage of 1200:1 – meaning 1200 minutes of waste (debt) for 1 minute of value-added (equity). In terms of value-adding capability, the company in this example is highly leveraged and will likely be distressed when economic conditions falter.

In past years, managers thought they were doing a good job if annual inventory turns were 3 or 5 (cost of goods sold divided by average inventory [for a given period]). In recent times, managers are quite happy with inventory turns of 8-12. Management's goal should be 50 inventory turns or better. So if annual inventory turns are 10, but could be 50 or better, then the leverage is 5:1 – meaning 5 inventory turns are wasted for every inventory turn that is actually achieved. In terms of inventory, the company in this example is highly leveraged and will likely be distressed when economic conditions falter. While numerically the leverage may appear to be small, the effect is huge. Large companies release tens of millions of dollars in cash with each additional inventory turn.

Most companies are also in heavy debt with respect to information; that is, information which is needed by people internally and externally but not provided in a timely basis or not provided at all. Conventional management is well known for requiring executives to contend with frequent unpleasant surprises. This is the result of disconnected processes, information hoarding, blocked information flows, etc. The debt of information internally is huge in part because workers and managers fear being blamed for problems. It is safer to tell management what it wants to hear: "There are no problems; we are on target for meeting our objectives."

The above examples are typical for a business that uses the batch-and-queue (B&Q) method to process material and information. B&Q puts the company deep into debt with respect to time, quantity, and information, and also financially because it must finance this inefficient and low-productivity production method with its own cash or with loans from banks. So despite an outward appearance of good financial performance, the company is actually in very bad shape – deep in many different types of debt. The question is, how do you get out of debt?

Whenever a company does well, top management's attention is usually directed to investors, while other stakeholders are generally ignored because they are assumed to be doing their job. However, when the company falters, the president or CEO invariably stresses the importance of key stakeholders – customers, employees, suppliers, communities, and even investors – and the need for their help in improving the company's financial condition. This situational embrace of stakeholders reveals management's insincerity, which undercuts teamwork in both good and bad times. A company needs its stakeholders all of the time in order to function effectively as a business. No exception.

One of the objectives of Lean management is to transform time, quantity, and information debt into equity by increasing productive capacity from within existing resources. That generates new capacity to produce innovative new products and services that will satisfy customer wants and needs, thus growing the business – which is what every top executive says they want to do [1]. The answer to the question of how do you get out of debt would seem to be simple: reduce lead-times, increase inventory turns, and get information to flow. But it is not so simple to do, and it takes people to make that happen.

Investors (e.g. large institutional investors) are the least capable of helping out because they are far removed from the company and their interests are very narrow. It takes the participation of insiders, employees, and closely-connected outsiders, suppliers, to do that [2]. However, if management's attention has previously focused on investors and ignored the other key stakeholders, then they will be less willing to participate. Management is now left with the difficult task of correcting its mistakes and regaining credibility among disenfranchised stakeholders.

The principal process for converting debt into equity is kaizen, which is a people-centered activity. Kaizen is a very powerful process which must be properly understood by executives (in detail) and correctly practiced. Developing a good understanding of kaizen comes in large part though direct participation in kaizen. Poorly executed kaizen does not convert debt into equity, so it is very important to get it right [3].

The people who participate in kaizen come from within the company; people from every department and at every level. They also come from outside the company, from upstream stakeholders such as suppliers, who usually own a part of lead-time, inventory, and information problems, as well as downstream stakeholders such as distributors or retailers. When kaizen is done well, people's brains, be they internal or external to the company, are used productively instead of being left fallow as is typically the case.

Employees are particularly important because they are the stakeholders closest to most problems. In addition to debt reduction, kaizen results in learning which expands and improves over time with daily exposure to kaizen. This is an attribute that is not appreciated by executives who have never participated in kaizen. In conducting kaizen, management is planting new seeds, which, if done well, will sprout, resulting in great enthusiasm for kaizen. This enthusiasm should be much-desired by management [4] because debt must be converted into equity on a daily basis, forever, not infrequently as is typically done (e.g. sporadic kaizen "events"). And the new sprouts must be allowed to grow and mature.

However, kaizen as it is commonly conducted results in employee layoffs, which is a huge mistake and reveals how little executives understand the process and intent of kaizen. Executives who uproot the saplings cut-off learning and turn kaizen into a process that harms people. If a process harms people, then you can expect, with 100 percent certainty, that people will not work together to reduce debt, leaving the company forever vulnerable. Similarly, if kaizen is used to harm the interests of suppliers or retailers, then they will not work with the company to reduce shared debts. People's brains will be wasted to satisfy management's knee-jerk short-term interests, which will make it difficult to grow the business.

It is easy to forget that debt of any type is bad because it masks volatility and dampens response to changing economic conditions. Executives have as part of their responsibilities to reduce debt (risk) and that takes people working together to achieve common objectives. Pulling out saplings will leave a company forever in debt because people will not work together.

Notes

[1] They should strive for stable long-term growth, and not inflate growth short-term to satisfy stock market analysts. They are not cash-paying customers.

[2] This will require most managers to change their school-yard attitude about suppliers, from an adversary to bully to much needed and helpful business partners. Not putting these brains to good use shows the extent to which management does not know how to utilize available external resources. See B. Emiliani, *Practical Lean Leadership: A Strategic Leadership Guide for Executives*, The CLBM, LLC, Wethersfield, Conn., 2008.

[3] See M. Imai, *Kaizen*, Random House, New York, NY, 1986; M. Imai, *Gemba Kaizen*, McGraw-Hill, New York, NY, 1997; and B. Emiliani, with D. Stec, L. Grasso, and J. Stodder, *Better Thinking, Better Results: Case Study and Analysis of an Enterprise-Wide Lean Transformation*, second edition, The CLBM, LLC, Wethersfield, Conn., 2007.

[4] Lower-level people who are enthusiastic about kaizen, and Lean management in general, can be viewed by managers who seek to preserve current management practices as disloyal and working against the company's interests. This, of course, is a false characterization meant to diminish people who promote progressive management principles and practices.

5 Change Your World

Almost every senior management team will hire a big-name consulting company to do what they are fully capable of doing themselves. The help received from consultants to implement Lean management may meet or exceed expectations in the beginning, but over time it will come to be seen as inadequate. Instead of depending on others, have confidence in yourself and all employees to think differently, do good work, and become self-reliant. To do this, you will need to change your world in at least two ways: 1) as defined by the limits of your mind, the result of years of acceptance of illogical arguments; and 2) with respect to your company and areas of responsibility.

Senior managers must question illogical arguments that they have accepted, such as viewing manual factory or service work as being less important than so-called knowledge work. All forms of manual work require deep knowledge to do the job right – think of the work of a dentist, a carpenter, a mechanic, or a musician. If you think that manufacturing is inferior to design, then you would agree that clinical medicine is inferior to medical research. You would agree that community banking is inferior to Wall Street financial engineering. You would agree construction is inferior to architecture. In all cases, you would be wrong. Both types of work need to be coupled, not de-coupled, to accumulate useful knowledge and capabilities, to assure the integrity of feedback, and to continuously improve the business system.

Disrespecting value-creating work – manufacturing and service operations – and the people who do it is stupid, and you will surely pay for such short-sightedness. You must think for yourself and reject illogical arguments.

Changing your world also means personal involvement in making improvements in your areas of responsibility. Start with business processes that are within your control to gain experience applying Lean principles and practices, being very careful not to negatively impact upstream or downstream processes. Then take the next step forward to connect business processes between departments and between your company and your suppliers and customers, to gain more experience at applying Lean principles and practices.

You will have done truly great work if that is all that you ever do. And you will have done it all on your own.

Make or Buy Lean?

*You won't find too many advocates of do-it-yourself Lean.
Nevertheless, executives should seriously consider it as a
viable alternative to the defective consultant-led approach to
a Lean transformation. Becoming self-reliant offers wide-
ranging personal and business rewards for decades
to come. It's well worth the effort.*

A major feature of Toyota's management practice is to rely on
one's self rather than relying on others for ideas, assistance,
fixing problems, money, etc. Former Toyota president Taizo
Ishida said: "Defend your own castle yourself... You defend
your company without reliance on others" [1]. For the most
part, that is what Toyota Motor Corporation has done for
decades. It did not hire a consultant to make the company
Lean [2], Toyota people did it themselves. In doing so, management learned the importance of the two bedrock principles
of Lean management: "Continuous Improvement" and
"Respect for People."

In contrast, companies today that wish to practice Lean management immediately look for an expensive big-name consultant to lead their Lean transformation efforts [3]. While
this surely delights consultants, the executive team has made
its first serious error in its fledgling Lean transformation: not
using the brains of its people at any level. The executives
delegate Lean implementation to a consultant who is expected to drive the necessary culture change [4]. As a result,
management never learns the importance of the "Respect for
People" principle.

If you decide to buy the consultant's service, then you should be very aware of what you are buying. When you hire a consultant to lead your Lean transformation, in most cases you will be procuring a defective service. Lean consultants sell only the tools of continuous improvement, often under the guise of a management system. They focus on the tools of continuous improvement because that's what sells, regardless of if it lacks completeness. This is true throughout the history of progressive management [5].

In general, consultants do not understand or care about the "Respect for People" principle – even though it is what makes Lean work – because it does not sell to executives. If they do offer some training, it will be a quick, high-level overview of the "Respect for People" principle, typically only in the context of employees [6]. They will leave out suppliers, customers, investors, and communities because they do not understand, or have very shallow understanding, of how the "Respect for People" principle relates to these key stakeholders. The same goes for trainers and educators, but not for historians who have studied the evolution of Lean management [7]. They know the "Respect for People" principle is not optional.

If you still want to buy the consultant's service, then you should demand a discount because you are buying seconds. The money you save should be put aside to pay for the future re-work you will have to do when you finally realize that the consultant did not (or could not) share with you what it really takes to make Lean work.

You may say: "Well, what if we hire a consultant just to teach

us a specific Lean tool such as policy deployme[
stream mapping, or A3 reports?" That sounds quite reason-
able – until you recognize that the tools cannot be correctly
understood or practiced in the absence of the "Respect for
People" principle. That testifies to the fundamental importance of the "Respect for People" principle.

When it comes to Lean management, it is much better to
make Lean yourself than to buy it. But to make it means that
every manager must participate in and practice Lean, CEO on
down. The job description of every manager must change to
include teaching Lean to others. Everyone will know management is serious about Lean when they see executives participating in kaizen, applying Lean principles and practices
every day, and teaching others about Lean.

But how will top executives learn about Lean management?
The answer to that question is to look at how Toyota managers created their management system:

1) They were highly dissatisfied with the current state of
   high costs, long-lead-times, large inventories, lack of
   flow, daily firefights, customer dissatisfaction, as well
   as their own knowledge and capabilities.
2) Learn from others: they read books and papers written
   by progressive industrial management practitioners
   (not theorists) including Frederick Taylor, Frank
   Gilbreth, Henry Ford, and likely Frank Woollard [8].
3) Use your own ideas: they had some good ideas of
   their own, including autonomation (jidoka), pull, and
   kanban [9].
4) Put their ideas and the ideas of others into practice.

5) Understand what worked and why.
6) Understand what did not work and why.
7) Determine root causes, implement countermeasures, and evaluate the results.
8) Standardize and improve each process [10].
9) Share the improvements across the company.

You can do exactly the same thing, no consultant is needed. You might want to talk to a Lean historian to expand your understanding of the nuances surrounding the whats and whys of Lean management, to remove confusion and doubts and to better explain Lean to others [5, 11]. However, you are clearly responsible for the hows (the process and results), not a consultant.

If you follow these nine steps, you too will learn the importance of the two bedrock principles of Lean management: "Continuous Improvement" and "Respect for People." The outcomes on a personal level include:

- You will be a better educated manager.
- You will expand your practical skills and capabilities.
- The errors that you make will be fewer and less severe.
- You will have less stress and more fun at work.

The outcomes on organizational and business levels include:

- Showing that management has confidence in themselves and in every employee to learn and improve.
- Greater employee involvement, specifically in identifying and correcting problems without the need for

management intervention.

- Less re-work, less firefighting, and dramatically improved information flow.
- Improved employee satisfaction, including higher base wages with the money that has been saved and through profit sharing [12].
- Reduced costs and improved responsiveness to changing market conditions.
- Improved competitiveness, in part due to the uniqueness of thinking and daily practices.

You will have to work harder for several years and you must be persistent, just as a new musician or a golfer would be, until you start to get it [13]. Difficulties will arise periodically and the demands on your time will increase, testing your abilities and commitment.

Making Lean yourself means that high-value practical skills will develop in the management team that an expensive Lean consultant can never provide [14].

Notes

[1] "The Toyota Way 2001," Toyota Motor Corporation, internal document, Toyota City, Japan, April 2001, p. 4

[2] Shigeo Shingo was not hired by Toyota to create Toyota's production system. He was hired by Toyota in late 1955 through October 1980 for the specific purpose of teaching basic industrial engineering methods (i.e. Taylor and Gilbreth) and their application in kaizen to engineers and supervisors in manufacturing. This training for ~3000 people supported the further development of Toyota's production system but was not central to it. See Art Smalley's interview of Isao Kato, "Mr. Shigeo Shingo's P-Course and Contribution to TPS," July 2006, http://www.superfactory.com/articles/featured/2006/0607-smalley-shingo-pcourse-tps.html. See also "A Brief Investigation Into the Origins of the Toyota Production System," Art Smalley, June 2006, http://www.superfactory.com/articles/featured/2006/Smalley_Origins_and_Facts_Regarding_TPS.pdf

[3] In their eagerness to hire a Lean consultant, most top executives rely on recommendations from their peers. They normally do not use the company's established request for information (RFI) or request for quote (RFQ) process, which is likely in violation of the company's procurement policy. Using the established purchasing process should allow greater opportunity to specify sources that truly understand the two principles of Lean management.

[4] Culture change will never occur this way. The beliefs, behaviors, and competencies of senior managers must change first, which then leads to changes in beliefs, behaviors, and competencies in people at lower levels. See B. Emiliani, *Practical Lean Leadership: A Strategic Leadership Guide for Executives*, The CLBM, LLC, Wethersfield, Conn., 2008

[5] See B. Emiliani, *REAL LEAN: Critical Issues and Opportunities in Lean Management*, Volume Two, The CLBM, LLC, Wethersfield, Conn., 2007, Chapters 1-6 and 10 and B. Emiliani, *REAL LEAN: The Keys to Sustaining Lean Management*, Volume Three, The CLBM, LLC, Wethersfield, Conn., 2008, Chapter 1

[6] See B. Emiliani, *REAL LEAN: The Keys to Sustaining Lean Management*, Volume Three, The CLBM, LLC, Wethersfield, Conn., 2008, Appendix 1, "The Equally Important Respect for People Principle."

[7] The perspective of a Lean historian is to study the factors that contribute to success and failures, and also look for recurring themes or trends. The application or non-application of the "Respect for People" principle (or its equivalent) is clear in the historical record, with the former consistently contributing to success. This differs greatly from consultants, trainers, or

educators (academics), whose interest is almost exclusively on the present and will therefore focus mainly on the "Continuous Improvement" principle. See note [5].

[8] See for example: F.W. Taylor, *The Principles of Scientific Management*, Harper & Brothers Publishers, New York, NY, 1911; F.B. Gilbreth, *Motion Study: A Method for Increasing the Efficiency of the Workman*, D. Van Nostrand Company, New York, NY, 1911; H. Ford with S. Crowther, *My Life and Work*, Garden City Publishing Company Inc., Garden City, NY, 1922; H. Ford with S. Crowther, *Today and Tomorrow*, Doubleday, Page & Company, New York, NY, 1926; F.G. Woollard, with B. Emiliani, *Principles of Mass and Flow Production*, 55th Anniversary Special Reprint Edition, The CLBM, LLC, Wethersfield, Conn., January 2009. You should read these old works because they are relevant to today's challenges. Key current-day Lean management authors today include: M.L. (Bob) Emiliani, Takahiro Fujimoto Daniel Jones, Jeffrey Liker, Brian Maskell, Yasuhiro Monden, Taiichi Ohno, and James Womack. Note that the "Respect for People" principal is consistently presented in Emiliani's books and papers, but less so, in varying degrees, for the other authors.

[9] Just-in-Time was in use long ago in the early U.S. and U.K. auto industries. Kiichiro Toyoda may have gotten the idea for JIT from visits to U.S. and U.K. automakers in 1929-1930, or it could have been arrived at independently. See M. Schwartz and A. Fish, "Just-in-Time Inventories in Old Detroit," *Business History*, Vol. 40, No. 3, 1998, pp. 48-71, and F.G. Woollard with B. Emiliani, *Principles of Mass and Flow Production*, 55th Anniversary Special Reprint Edition, The CLBM, LLC, Wethersfield, Conn., January 2009.

[10] People widely misunderstand the word "standardize" in the phrase "standardized work." They think it means to find the one best way to do a process and then do that process the same way forever. This is incorrect. Standardized work is the agreed upon best known way to do a job at a point in time, and is revised often, as soon as new ideas are generated to improve the process or if there are changes in equipment, personnel, customer demand, etc. Standardized work is never meant to be static.

[11] B. Emiliani, *REAL LEAN: The Keys to Sustaining Lean Management*, Volume Three, The CLBM, LLC, Wethersfield, Conn., 2008

[12] Use a simple profit sharing formula such as: 15% of pre-tax consolidated income divided by total straight time wages for the quarter. See B. Emiliani, with D. Stec, L. Grasso, and J. Stodder, *Better Thinking, Better Results: Case Study and Analysis of an Enterprise-Wide Lean Transformation*, second edition, The CLBM, LLC, Wethersfield, Conn.,

2007, pp. 124-126

[13] See B. Emiliani, *REAL LEAN: Learning the Craft of Lean Management*, Volume Four, The CLBM, LLC, Wethersfield, Conn., 2008.

[14] I have always greatly favored making things myself whenever possible. Here are some examples: When I was 15, I decided to process my black & white and color film in my own darkroom. I learned a lot more than if I simply took my rolls of film to a Fotomat store. When I was 17, I decided to build my own high-end custom racing bicycle frames, starting with building jigs in metal shop during my senior year in high school. The first frame I built was a big success. I learned a lot more than if I simply bought a custom racing bicycle. When I was 37, I decided to create my own works of art. I created unique works of art and developed new concepts and techniques in art that had never been done before. I learned a lot more than if I simply bought artwork made by others or visited museums. When I was 45, I decided to put my knowledge and practical experiences in Lean management to use by writing books about Lean management – creative and original works that focused on leadership and other aspects of Lean management that nobody else covered. I learned a lot more than if I simply bought books written by others. When I was 45, I decided to make music by learning how to play the bass guitar. It was my most challenging activity ever, yet I taught myself 90+ songs and have begun to compose songs. I learned a lot more than if I simply bought CDs and listened to them. When I was 47, I decided to make my own garden-fresh pasta sauce, fruit jams, roasted peppers, and marinated roasted hot peppers. I learned a lot more than if I simply went to a specialty grocer and bought commercially processed foods. My message to you is simple: Rise to the challenge, do the work, and make Lean yourself! You will learn 100,000 times more than if you pay consultants to implement Lean for you.

6 Final Thoughts

While the benefits of REAL LEAN management are many and proven, companies will never be able to access them if executives remain disengaged and are satisfied with Fake Lean – defective variants of Lean in which tools have been cherry-picked and the "Respect for People" principle is unrecognized or has been discarded.

This book offers a set of five broad strategies to executives for achieving REAL LEAN management success.

- Pay Attention to History
- Learn From Others
- See Reality
- Work Together
- Change Your World

While some details were covered, there are many more details still to learn. Some of these details are presented in the other books that I have written and in books written by Takahiro Fujimoto, Masaaki Imai, Jeffrey Liker, Brian Maskell, Yasuhiro Monden, as well as in books published by Productivity Press and the Lean Enterprise Institute.

The remaining details are perhaps the most important because they represent tacit knowledge that can only be learned through direct participation in the application of Lean principles and practices. Lean requires managers at all levels to improve their practical intelligence, derived not from theoretical studies but from daily experience: e.g. genchi genbutsu, kaizen, etc.

There is also the matter of the often neglected "Respect for People" principle. Throughout the history of progressive management, the pioneers started out by forcing their brilliant new ideas onto the workplace. Each one learned the same lesson the hard way: that improvement cannot be zero-sum (win-lose), yielding positive results for the company but at the expense of employees or other key stakeholders. Realizing their mistake, they modified their approach to be non-zero-sum (win-win), where the company and its key stakeholders benefit from process improvements. That is when they experienced real success.

Executives, who, over the decades have tried to replicate the success of the pioneers, almost always follow the far more disruptive zero-sum path, primarily because that is what they are used to doing. They incorrectly think that the same rules and practices for leadership apply in conventional management as they do in progressive Lean management. The "Respect for People" principle is the banana peel on the floor that executives always find a way to slip on. Employees, representing one key stakeholder group, will predictably resist that which offers no benefits to them. It is a simple cause-and-effect relationship that, amazingly, most executives prefer to ignore.

Another way to look at the common problem of zero-sum improvement is to consider the question: "What do we want employees to be thinking about at work?" Do you want them thinking about:

- Wage stagnation
- Benefits cutbacks
- Unclear expectations

- Organizational politics and blame
- Maximizing shareholder value

Or do you want them thinking about:

- Recognizing problems
- Doing formal root cause analysis
- Identifying and implementing countermeasures
- Improving processes in every department and between departments
- Developing innovative products and services that grow sales.

You should want all employees' attention focused on the latter, but that will not happen if your leadership is rigidly centered on zero-sum thinking and outcomes (which obstructs flow). You can lead in ways that do not distract employees so they will be focused on doing their job, taking initiative, and improving the workplace every day. That means you must be proactive in removing that which dissatisfies employees, so that improvement is seen by employees and others as a non-zero-sum activity, and inspiring them to improve by leading by example.

Appendix I – The Growth Imperative

The top executives of companies, particularly large companies whose shares are traded on stock exchanges, always emphasize the need for sales growth – often at very aggressive rates that are much higher than industry average. Executives say things like: "If you're not growing, then you are going backwards" or "Grow or die." They are expressing the growth imperative, which means to increase sales and profits every year without interruption.

From a practical standpoint, this is not possible due to changes micro-economic conditions (e.g. poor-selling products, new competition, etc.) and macro-economic conditions (e.g. recessions). Nevertheless, the growth imperative, "grow or die," is taken as gospel and management teams try very hard to achieve year-over-year increase sales and profits.

Is it really true that if you do not grow you will die, or if you're not growing then you are going backwards? Why is growth so important to a company? Who is asking the company to grow; customers, suppliers, investors? Usually it is investors, a special interest group, whose narrow desires can greatly disrupt the interests of other stakeholders and the ability of the company to satisfy customers.

In natural living systems, things grow, decline or flat-line when stressed, grow again, and then decline and eventually die. While nobody wants to see a company die, why isn't the combination of growth, flat-line or decline, and re-growth more accepted as a natural consequence of economic activity? Why should sales growth be exempt from periodic declines? Permanent economic growth is unrealistic.

Why is sales growth important and what does it do?

- Makes a company more valuable, assuming profitable growth.
- Allows the company to pay off debts.
- Makes a company harder to take over because it is more expensive to buy.
- Strengthens competitiveness.
- Creates jobs (maybe).
- Increases incomes (for some).
- Helps the company survive.
- Influential people say growth is important.

Growth, however, does not offer only upside benefits. It can also cause many problems:

- Hide systemic and day-to-day problems.
- Can sacrifice future long-term growth to achieve short-term growth.
- Managers seek economies of scale and completely ignore diseconomies of scale (see Section 1, "Toyota's British Influence").
- Compels managers to diversify into lines of business where risks are poorly understood and details of the business are not well known.
- Difficulty digesting acquisitions and realizing synergies, and corporate culture clashes.
- Managers game the metrics to achieve appearance of growth (e.g. channel stuffing).
- Reduce competition (temptation to create sellers' mar-

kets and gain pricing power).

- Take advantage of customers who have less choice.
- Focus becomes getting people to buy things they don't need (resulting in higher SG&A expenses and likelihood of flat or declining wages and benefits as non-wage costs increase).
- Trains people over the long-term to do the things that are required to grow sales, and therefore have the wrong skill set when decline inevitably comes (e.g. recession).
- Complacency.

Organic growth or growth through acquisition of product lines or companies is expensive. There is uncertainty in budgeting for internal growth, and management usually overpays for acquisitions. So large debts are usually incurred and paying off debts is a major reason why growth is needed. However, the company would not have debt if it lived within its means, just as you and I must do in our personal lives. Did management save enough money to internally finance growth, or did they distribute most of the profits to shareholders over the years, requiring them to go to banks for loans to finance growth?

It turns out that even a relatively modest 7% compound annual growth rate (CAGR) can get companies into a lot of trouble, as happened to Toyota Motor Corporation (1998-2008), let alone CAGRs of 20-30% or more sought by many companies (e.g. DaimlerChrysler, Enron, Tyco, Duke Energy, the sub-prime lending industry, etc.). Rapid growth is a principal cause of corporate distress. If growth is imperative, then management should have a conservative growth strategy, a well-understood growth processes, and execute growth very carefully.

Businesses that convert from batch-and-queue to Lean quickly gain new capacity from existing resources. Management can either cut capacity and lay people off to put costs in-line with current sales volumes, which would be a mistake, or they can grow the business – which is what almost all executives say they want to do. To absorb the new-found capacity in production and productivity gains in that and other departments without layoffs, a company will have to grow at 10-20% CAGR. Cash flow will increase due to reductions in inventories and the time that it takes to process goods and services. So there is money to invest in organic growth or to buy product lines or companies.

These are potentially wonderful developments, but where there is opportunity there is also risk. Double-digit CAGRs, while seductive, can be dangerous, perhaps not immediately, but surely some years later on. In addition, management and employees seem to be better at practicing Lean management under conditions of growth rather than decline, exposing weaknesses in management capabilities in down markets.

On the other hand, periods of flat growth or decline can be beneficial because they offer new opportunities such as:

- Expose problems.
- Lead to improvements in organizational routines.
- People learn new things.
- Apply existing skills to new problems.
- Promote the development of new skills that well-

rounded leaders should possess.

The practice of Lean management offers valuable opportunities to learn and improve in all parts of the business cycle. Further, growth should not be forced simply to satisfy the narrow interests of a single stakeholder. Management should educate investors on the danger of double-digit CAGRs.

Stable long-term growth is the preferred objective, which implies a CAGR of 2-4% – with most or all of that growth being organic. That is not as glamorous as 10-20% or more CAGRs generated principally by acquisitions, but the potential for future organizational and financial distress is greatly reduced.

This also suggests the need for a more balanced approach to the Lean transformation, in which the pace of improvement in operations is diminished and the pace of improvement in other functional areas is increased. In other words, change the historical pattern of Lean transformations from narrow and deep (i.e. operations-focused) to more broad but shallower across the enterprise. And pace yourself.

This will result in more balanced improvement across the entire enterprise, while a less aggressive CAGR will enable the executive team and employees respond more effectively to the challenges associated with sales growth and profitability.

Appendix II – Lean Writing & Publishing

For over a decade my writing has focused on answering one simple question:

> "What aspects of Lean management do managers
> not understand?"

In answering that question [1], I purposely sought to add originality to Lean thinking and practice that has been lacking, while at the same time making sure that what I develop is simple, easy to understand, easy to remember, and easy to put into practice. Most books on Lean management report what Toyota does, and the authors offer little in the way of their own original and creative inputs. While these books can be very valuable, most do not concisely capture critical information that executives need.

In addition, the processes of writing and publishing are batch-and-queue and thus in great need of improvement. We know from experience with Lean management that its principles and practices apply to just about every business, but does it apply to writing and book publishing? Of course it does. While I have made efforts to improve my writing and publishing processes, they do remain mainly batch-and-queue – though it has been lightly hybridized with Lean principles and some Lean practices. I have not been able to do better than that so far.

How do Lean principles and practices apply to the process of writing and producing a book? Let's start with the principles. Table 1 summarizes how I apply the two Lean principles, "Continuous Improvement" and "Respect for People," to my writing and the book production process:

Table 1

Lean Principle	Application to Writing and Publishing
Continuous Improvement	• Practice writing, idea generation, or organizing book thoughts and ideas every day. • Read a wide range of different subject matter daily. • Proof read more thoroughly, and in different settings (I'm trying a pub lately, the Twin Willows in Narragansett, RI). • Be responsive to reviewer feedback; make changes or edit/re-write to clarify points being made. • Learn from the copy editor, graphic artist, and printer/distributor. • Provide specific and actionable feedback to the copy editor, graphic artist, and printer/distributor. • Use new print-on-demand technology (starting in fall 2002), rather than large run printing + inventorying books.
Respect for People	• Respect the reader and other stakeholders; understand their needs and perspectives. Supply practical information; leave theory to others. • Produce products for which there is demand, but sometimes may have to lead the market. • Respect the reader's time; be direct and get to the point. • Keep costs low and value high. Eschew fancy book covers and fancy graphics; produce only paperback editions. Keep things simple. • Price books at low end to extend reach for helping people to better understand and improve their practice of Lean management. • Understand the work requirements of the copy editor, graphic artist, and printer/distributor. • Develop and maintain good relationship with book printer/distributor, and direct customers. • Pay suppliers on-time; sooner is better.

I do not claim that I do these things perfectly. In som
I am in need of substantial improvement. In additioı., ı am
sure I have not yet thought of important things that I should
be doing.

David M. Miller pointed out in his review of *REAL LEAN:
Understanding the Lean Management System* (Volume One),
posted on amazon.com, that I can improve my practice of the
"Respect for People," where people in this case are readers.
Mr. Miller said:

> "He [Emiliani] approaches his writing in an 'I'm
> right, you're wrong' type [of] attitude (which is
> clearly zero-sum thinking)…"

This is a very interesting criticism, one that caused me to
think quite a bit about my viewpoint as an author and my style
of writing the *REAL LEAN* series of books. My tone can
indeed be sharp at times, but the purpose of that is to be clear
and not equivocate. Do I have an "I'm right, you're wrong"
attitude? It is not a case of "I'm right, you're wrong." My
research on the history and evolution of Lean management
clearly reveals principles, practices, and ways of thinking that
have empirically proved themselves to be better. It is the pioneers who succeeded with progressive management in the
real world who are right, not me. The criticism is good and
helped me recognize that I need to be more clear on this point.

So how does the book writing process get started? The image
below shows the raw material that I begin my writing process
with. It is a bunch of ideas that I write down whenever they
come to me, day or night, while exercising, practicing my

bass guitar, cooking, cleaning, driving – whenever.

I collect these ideas in a folder, typically, but not always, pertaining to a specific book topic or chapter I hope to write in the future. The ideas are collected for several months. I periodically read each note to judge if it still has merit. I ask myself:

- Is it a useful thought?
- It is profound, original, or creative?
- How can it be improved?
- Does it help explain or clarify something useful?
- Would managers benefit from knowing about this?
- Does it relate to the real world?
- It is specific, practical, or actionable?

I save the good ideas and toss out the bad ideas. I start writing when the ideas begin to gel, which usually occurs suddenly. I get excited and become highly motivated to write. Often I don't really know where to start, so I just get started and within 10 or 20 minutes I know where I am headed. I rarely listen to music when I write, no cigar smoking, and no drinking coffee or booze. I just write – 2 to 5 hours at a sit-ting, some days for 10 to 12 hours. Writing to me is a bench assembly process, but is also a flow experience (i.e. time flies) that I like very much.

Each idea is transferred into a Microsoft Word file and grouped together according to the thoughts I want to develop. My initial manuscript for each chapter will be 1 or 2 pages long containing a series of disconnected thoughts and sentences. I then develop each one of them and write introductory paragraphs to introduce the topic. Sometimes the ideas are re-ordered, but not too often.

I never work from a formal outline because my ideas are either well formulated at the start of this process or are quickly adjusted as I write. Perhaps I am combining the creation of an outline and writing at the same time. I have never had writer's block in more than 30 years of writing articles, journal papers, and books. The words have always flowed easily, in part because I think I am well prepared when I begin to write, having spent a lot of time reading, practicing Lean, and thinking prior to writing.

Only once did I use a formal outline, but it was not the type of outline you or I used in grade school. It was a detailed PowerPoint presentation that I worked on for over a year to explore and answer the question of why managers have so much difficulty sustaining Lean management. That became the outline for *REAL LEAN: The Keys to Sustaining Lean Management* (Volume Three). Interestingly, the process of writing the book revealed small logic problems in the PowerPoint slides, which I then corrected.

My first drafts have always been about 90% on-target (a high first-pass yield), and thus requiring minor editing. Rarely will I have to totally re-write more than a paragraph or two. The manuscripts for the *REAL LEAN* books are produced in about three weeks. Then I spend a week or two reading the manuscript several times and making thousands of small edits to ensure I am saying exactly what I mean to say. I am careful to make sure I select the words that best reflect my meaning and intent. All of this work is part-time, sandwiched between the courses I teach, daily bass guitar practice, yard work, cooking dinners, parenting, etc.

The next step is copy editing, which is where I always get a rude awakening. I am amazed to see the number of typos I have generated on each page. My copy editor, Mary Milewski, does not re-write my work; she corrects it and lets my

writing style come through. Copy editing generally takes a couple of weeks. We meet face-to-face to go over the copy edited manuscript page-by-page to ensure I understand every one of her edits. I incorporate the changes within a day or two.

The manuscript then goes to the graphic artist to create the book layout, line drawings, images, etc. Tom Bittel and I sit down and go over the manuscript page by page. The manuscript is marked-up to call attention to various special requirements. About three weeks later, the first draft of the book arrives for examination. The corrected draft is returned to Tom and the process is repeated one or two more times over the next week or two.

Once the layout is complete, I produce the index. This is a tedious and time-consuming task, but people who use Indexes a lot appreciate it when they are done well. Also, I know I am near the end of the process when the index file is done and sent to Tom to incorporate into the book file.

Tom delivers the cover and book pages in .pdf files saved according to the printer's specifications. I upload the title information and book files to the printer's Web site. The operations supervisor, Rachel, examines the files and notifies me if they are in good order or if they need to be corrected. If the files are good, a proof copy of the book arrives within a few days for me to review and approve. If the proof is good, I approve it and the book is released into the marketplace.

Lead-time for each volume of the *REAL LEAN* books, once writing begins, is about 95 days (1,520 hours over two part-time shifts) while the value-added time is about 170 hours, with about 90% of that time being the consumed by the author in writing and several rounds of editing prior to copy editing, post-copy editing editing, and 2-3 rounds of reviewing and correcting the book pages prior to it being sent to the printer. The lead-time with a big-name corporate publisher is typically 3-4 times longer, about 9-12 months, while the value added time is about the same.

That is a general summary of the process, which is a big improvement over corporate publishing, but it can still be further improved. A value stream map illustrating my book writing and publishing process is shown on the facing page. The current state is a batch process, primarily because of the large mismatch in cycle times for each step in the process.

Please note that once the proof is approved, the process changes from batch-and-queue to Lean for selling and printing books. All of my books are print-on-demand titles; the customer orders from amazon.com, for example, who then pulls from a small supermarket and re-orders more books from the printer when supply is depleted. It is not a perfect pull system, but it is surely better than the old way of printing thousands of copies, keeping them in inventory, pushing the books onto bookstores, discounting to drive sales, crediting the bookstore when unsold books are returned, and then destroying the over-production. The rapid trend towards e-books will result in a more effective pull system for fulfilling sales orders, but not for writing and publishing.

The next question is, how do Lean practices apply to the process of writing and producing a book? This is where it gets a bit tougher. Since writing and publishing are batch-and-queue, few

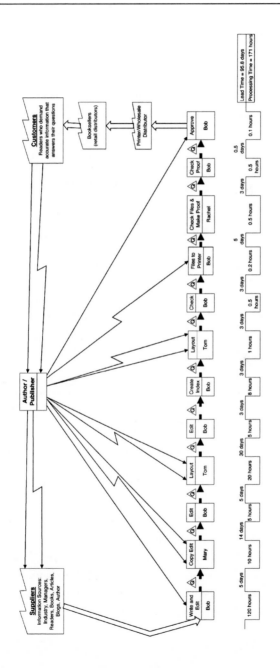

Lean practices and tools apply. Table 2 summarizes how I apply selected Lean practices to writing and book production:

Table 2

Lean Practice	Application to Writing and Publishing
Five S	• Document ideas by keeping notes. • Keep notes organized and in safe place. • Review notes periodically and re-classify, edit, or discard bad or irrelevant ideas.
Just-in-Time	• Respond to actual demand of readers for the information they need. • Produce books that are responsive to current and emerging needs of readers for practical information.
Heijunka	• Write or edit every day.
Autonomation	• Computerized word processing with automatic spelling correction and grammar check.
Standardized Work	• Follow established work sequence (see value stream map) • Standard format for most books and chapters.
Teamwork	• Do things to help copy editor and graphic artist succeed in their work. • Meet face-to-face.

Note that I do not work to a takt time (e.g. 2 pages per day), and so standardized work is not practiced in the same way as in Lean management. Also, it is less clear on how visual controls can be used, other than by scheduling work activities. While some Lean practices and tools can be applied, others do not seem to fit well. That is how I see it now, but I am sure that the ways in which Lean tools and processes can be applied will become clearer as I think more about it.

Appendix II

Notes

[1] A main tenet of Lean management is to see reality
tenet, which I learned on day one of my Lean trainin
has always guided my writing. The result is that I blun
agement, which can make some executives feel uncom
sonally offended. I know this because I periodically get feedback that says
I could "attract more bees with honey." In other words, if I sugar coat reality then more people would read my books. My experience has been that
the sugar coated approach as well as the direct approach I use in my books
are imperfect and each has limitations. In general, managers, like any
human, filter out what they do not like or pump in more of what they do
like, regardless of the approach employed by the writer. I chose to be consistent with Lean principles and practices and just present the naked realities, knowing that managers' filters and pumps are not in my control.
Nearly all non-profit and for-profit organizations that promote Lean management sugar coat reality in different ways and to different extents. This
makes their customers think that Lean management is easier to practice
than it really is, which is misleading. They do this mainly to perpetuate
their self-interests. My situation is different; I maintain full-time employ-
ment as a university professor so I do not have to perpetuate my self-interest. Therefore, I tell it like it is. My pain is your gain. Organizations that
sugar coat the personal and organizational challenges of Lean management
lose credibility and force people to do re-work when managers finally
become aware of the realities. Most managers do not like to engage in re-
work, especially if they must confess that they misunderstood something
from the start. As a result, senior managers will typically allow the practice
of Lean management to stumble along or let it slowly fade away, replacing
it with a new "program" or "initiative." The problem with sugar coating
reality is that it sets managers up to fail and is inconsistent with the
"Respect for People" principle. If I tell senior managers the truth they may
decide to not adopt Lean management. That is their informed choice. Or,
they may decide to adopt Lean management realizing to a great degree
what they are committing themselves and their organizations to doing. The
sugar coated approach means that most managers will engage in Fake Lean
from the start and for many years thereafter, which is bad for all stakeholders. It also gives Lean a bad name, which, over time, will surely turn off
future generations of managers. If my writing personally offends you – if it
makes you realize that you are not a good manager – then perhaps I have
done a better job than if my writing did not offend you. It means I am close
to the truth. Instead of being upset with me, consider putting that negative

energy to good use: let it be the source of motivation for you to improve yourself and the organization.

Appendix III – Lean Mind, New Art

One genre of conventional visual art is paint on canvas. The only thing allowed is variations of paint colors, textures, and brushstrokes on a canvas, but it can sometimes include mixed media. The required form is paint on a 2-dimensional surface, whose overall size can vary widely. Dry paint means the artist's work is done.

A progressive artist asks new questions such as: "Can paint be removed from the canvas? How would you do that? What can you do with paint that has been removed from the canvas? What can such art look like? What can it communicate to people?" I explored these questions and created a new type of art, some examples of which are presented in the following pages. In this case, dry paint means the artist's work has just begun.

These works of art are a fusion of conceptual, minimalist, and abstract art forms. I call it "M3" art because three principal forms of modern visual art (post-World War II) have been merged. They represent a transformed image of the original paint on canvas image. One result is that the normally distinct boundaries between painting and sculpture have been blurred. The large 2-dimensional painted picture plane has been transformed irreversibly into small 3-dimensional works using different techniques.

My new art form questions many basic assumptions such as: 1) paintings must exist on planar surfaces, 2) paintings must be preserved, 3) the form or category of art informs the aesthetic, 4) the subject of the painting or other visual information is important for interpretation, 5) details contained in the painting aid in critical analysis, and 6) the technical painting skills of the artist and related factors matter. M3 art says each one of these assumptions is incorrect.

Casting off old assumptions makes M3 art provocative, interesting, and, most importantly, innovative. In addition, this new art form frees paintings from the wall, while its condensed volume can be displayed in a variety of new formats, alone or in combination.

Composition No. 7, 5 x 8 x 4 inches, 1998.
Photo of original painting on left (original size 24 x 36 inches).

Composition No. 18, 5 x 8 x 4 inches, 1999.
Photo detail of original painting on left (original size 24 x 36 inches).

Composition No. 10, 5 x 9 x 9 inches, 1999.
Photo of original painting on left (original size 24 x 36 inches).

Composition No. 16, 6 x 9 x 4 inches, 1999.
Photo detail of original painting on left (original size 24 x 36 inches).

Composition No. 37, 3.5 x 8 x 4 inches, 2000.
Original size 24 x 24 inches.

Composition No. 42 (left) and Composition No. 40 (right),
3.5 x 6 x 3.5 inches, 2000. Original sizes 24 x 36 inches.

Composition No. 29 (detail), 2 x 2.5 inches, 1999.
Original size 3 x 36 inches.

Composition No. 3 (detail), 4 x 4 x 4 inches, 1998.
Original size 24 x 36 inches.

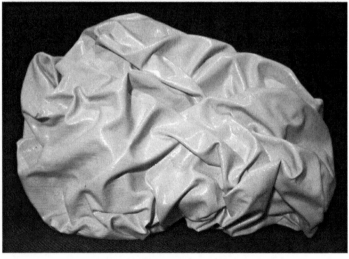

Composition No. 38, 6 x 8 x 2 inches, 2000.
Original size 24 x 36 inches.

Untitled, 24 x 36 inches, 2004. Ripped paint re-mounted on canvas.
Original size 14 x 32 inches.

"Now it's time to practice."

About the Author

M.L. "Bob" Emiliani is a professor at Connecticut State University in New Britain, Conn., where he teaches various courses on Lean management.

He worked in the consumer products and aerospace industries for nearly two decades and held management positions in engineering, manufacturing, and supply chain management, and had responsibility for implementing Lean in manufacturing operations and supply chains.

Emiliani has authored or co-authored a dozen papers related to Lean leadership including: "Lean Behaviors" (1998), "Linking Leaders' Beliefs to their Behaviors and Competencies" (2003), "Using Value Stream Maps to Improve Leadership" (2004), "Origins of Lean Management in America: The Role of Connecticut Businesses" (2006), and "Standardized Work for Executive Leadership" (2008). Five of his papers have won awards for excellence.

He is the principal author of the book *Better Thinking, Better Results: Case Study and Analysis of an Enterprise-Wide Lean Transformation*, (second edition, 2007), a detailed case study and analysis of The Wiremold Company's Lean transformation from 1991 to 2001. It won a Shingo Research Prize in 2003 as the first book to describe an enterprise-wide Lean transformation in a real company where both principles of Lean management – "Continuous Improvement" and "Respect for People" – were applied.

He is also the author of *REAL LEAN: Understanding the Lean Management System* (Volume One) and *REAL LEAN: Critical Issues and Opportunities in Lean Management* (Volume Two), both published in 2007, *REAL LEAN: The Keys to Sustaining Lean Management* (Volume Three), published in 2008, *REAL LEAN: Learning the Craft of Lean Management* (Volume Four), published in 2009, and *Practical Lean Leadership: A Strategic Leadership Guide For Executives*, published in 2008.

Emiliani has a B.S. in mechanical engineering from the University of Miami, M.S. in chemical engineering from the University of Rhode Island, and a Ph.D. in Engineering from Brown University.

He is the owner of The CLBM, LLC.
(www.bobemiliani.com).

Lightning Source UK Ltd.
Milton Keynes UK
20 February 2010

150407UK00001B/34/P